The Aliens Handbook

Herbie Brennan is a professional writer whose work has appeared in more than fifty countries. He began a career in journalism at the age of eighteen and when he was twenty-four became the youngest newspaper editor in his native Ireland.

By his mid-twenties, he had published his first novel, an historical romance brought out by Doubleday in New York. At age thirty, he made the decision to devote his time to full-length works of fiction for both adults and children. Since then he has published more than ninety books, many of them international best-sellers, for both adults and children.

Other books by Herbie Brennan
published by Faber & Faber

The Ghosthunter's Handbook

The Spy's Handbook

Space Quest
111 Peculiar Questions about the Universe and Beyond

The Aliens Handbook

Herbie Brennan

Illustrated by The Maltings Partnership

faber and faber

Illustrated by The Maltings Partnership

First published in 2005 by Faber and Faber Limited
3 Queen Square, London WC1N 3AU

Layout and typesetting by Planet Creative Ltd

Editorial: Paula Borton

Printed in England by Bookmarque Ltd

© Herbie Brennan, 2005

Herbie Brennan is hereby identified as author of this work in
accordance with Section 77 of the Copyright, Designs and Patents
Act 1988

A CIP record for this book is available from the British Library

The website addresses (URLs) included in this book are valid at
the time of going to press. However, because of the nature of the
Internet, it is possible that a site's address may have changed or
changed. While the author and publishers regret any inconvenience,
no responsibility can be accepted for such changes.

ISBN 0-571-22081-9

2 4 6 8 10 9 7 5 3 1

CONTENTS

To Isla, my favourite human.
From The Godfather

INTRODUCTION

Back in the 1940s, a few people reported seeing strange craft in the skies. These craft were usually described as saucer shaped and moved far faster than any known aeroplane. There were rumours that they might be spaceships. People suspected Earth was being visited by creatures from another planet. The authorities dismissed this as nonsense.

During the 1950s a handful of people -- mainly in North and South America – reported they'd been contacted by the aliens who flew flying saucers and told they should try to stop atom-bomb testing, which was widespread at the time. The authorities dismissed this as nonsense.

In 1961, an American couple reported that they had been abducted by flying-saucer aliens, who performed medical experiments on them before tinkering with their memories and allowing them to go. More abduction reports appeared over the next few years. The authorities dismissed this as nonsense.

Today there are records of Unidentified Flying Objects (UFOs or flying saucer) sightings that run into several hundred thousands. Many of the sightings have been caught on film, video or still photographs and experts are convinced the pictures are genuine. The objects they show are known to appear on radar and leave ground traces when they land. The trickle of abduction claims has turned into a flood. One highly qualified investigator estimates the number of abductees runs into *millions* in America alone. The

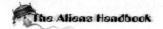

authorities *still* dismiss all this as nonsense.

Are you happy that the authorities are giving UFOs and alien abductions the attention they deserve? If not, this handbook is for you. It's divided into three sections. The first contains the straight facts about the whole phenomenon, the second deals with the more popular theories put forward to explain it and the third, most importantly, brings you the tools you need to investigate it for yourself.

Because if the authorities aren't doing anything after all this time, *somebody* needs to find out just what's going on.

PART ONE

The Facts

ONE

THE BEGINNING

World War Two, which broke out in 1939, was the first conflict in human history to make serious use of aircraft for military purposes. (Biplanes *did* take to the skies during World War One, but their contribution to the war effort consisted largely of a few dogfights – during some of these the pilots threw bricks at one another.)

From about 1942 onwards, Allied pilots (those fighting against the Nazis) increasingly began to report their planes were being tracked by small, disc-shaped objects capable of exceptional speeds and manoeuvrability. Although no planes were actually attacked, it was thought that the discs were a secret Nazi weapon, possibly some sort of spy craft. The pilots dreamed up a slang name for them – *foo fighters.*

Several attempts were made to shoot down a foo fighter, but without result: the craft moved too quickly. When the war ended in 1945, the victorious Allies searched carefully for Nazi secret weaponry. While it was clear that Germany was far advanced in its development of rocketry, the official records showed no sign at all of the foo fighters. But a search of captured documents soon showed that *Luftwaffe* (German Air Force) pilots reported being buzzed by flying discs too. They assumed they must be Allied secret weapons.

With the war over and a slow return to normality in Europe, people quickly forgot about the mysterious flying discs. Then something happened in America to bring them slap bang into the centre of public attention. In 1947, two years after the war in Europe ended, a transport plane crashed somewhere in Washington State. At that time, rescue operations were a lot less sophisticated than they are today and the number of available aircraft relatively small. Word went out to anyone who could help. Several amateur flyers volunteered to join in the search. Among them was Kenneth Arnold.

Kenneth Arnold was a businessman who flew light planes in his spare time. But amateur or not, he was still an experienced pilot. Reports indicated that apart from mistakes on take-off and landing, the most common cause of aircraft accidents during the 1940s was poor altitude judgement – the conviction that you are flying higher than you actually are. This sort of mistake can be particularly dangerous over mountainous terrain. Consequently, Arnold turned his aircraft towards the Cascade Range which he felt might be one of the more likely areas for the transport crash.

He headed for Mount Rainier. At 4,389 metres this is the highest mountain in the Cascades, some 64 kilometres (40 miles) southeast of Tacoma City. Rainier is the remnant of an ancient volcano and a large mountain by any standard. It covers approximately 259 square kilometres (100 square miles) and is surrounded by the largest single-mountain glacier system in the United States outside Alaska – an astounding 41 glaciers radiate from its summit. With three major peaks, it could prove hazardous for an unwary pilot.

As he watched out for signs of wreckage, Arnold must have admired the scenic beauty below him. There were dense woods of coniferous trees on the lower slopes of the mountain, flanked by alpine meadows, waterfalls and lakes – an environment that made the entire area a major tourist attraction. Then something happened that took his mind off both the scenery and his search. Nine disc-

shaped objects suddenly sped past his plane. They were flying in two parallel lines and flying fast.

Although familiar with most types of aircraft, Arnold had never seen anything like these. He swung his plane and opened up the throttle to get a closer look, but the discs continued to pull away from him. Using a process known as triangulation, he made a rough estimate of their speed ... then double-checked his figures since they appeared totally impossible. According to his calculations, the discs were moving at an incredible 2,574 kilometres (1,600 miles) per hour. This was not just faster than Arnold's own small single-engined plane, it was far faster than any other plane on Earth.

After a few minutes, Arnold gave up the chase, still no wiser about the nature of the strange craft. When he landed, he reported his sighting to Air Traffic Control, who were just as bewildered. Nobody made any immediate connection between the Mount Rainier discs and the foo fighters of Europe. Some time later, local newspapers got wind of the sighting and approached Kenneth Arnold for an interview. He described the way the discs flew as, 'like a saucer would if you skipped it across the water.' The press loved it. They headlined their newspapers with the new 'flying saucers'.

It was the start of something big. Following massive and widespread publicity about the Mount Rainier discs, more reports began to flow in. The bulk of these ended up with the United States Air Force and became so numerous that an investigation – code-named Project Sign – was established to try to find out what was going on.

To date, more than 50,000 worldwide sighting reports have been logged on computer – a figure generally accepted to represent the very small tip of a very large iceberg. By 1973 a survey indicated that 11% of the adult population of the United States had seen a UFO. This works out at some 20 million people. Some of them claim they actually saw one crash.

TWO

ONE CAME DOWN

On July 1, 1947 – the start of the Independence Day weekend in America – several unidentified flying objects showed up on the radar screens at the White Sands rocket testing grounds in New Mexico. Army personnel tried desperately to discover what was up there, but the UFOs eluded them.

On the evening of July 2, Mr and Mrs Dan Wilmot were sitting on their porch in the nearby town of Roswell when they saw something mysterious pass overhead.

On the night of Independence Day itself (July 4), a local rancher, Mac Brazel, heard an explosion so loud it drowned out the noise of the thunderstorm that was taking place. At around the same time, a White Sands radar object went starburst – an effect usually taken to indicate a crash.

Meanwhile, north of Roswell, Jim Ragsdale and his girlfriend, Trudy Truelove, watched a glowing object pass over their campsite before crashing about 1 1/2 kilometres (1 mile) away. The couple drove across rough terrain to find out what had happened and eventually came across a strange-looking object lying against the side of a cliff. As they walked towards it, their electric torch suddenly failed. Unable to find their way in the darkness, they returned to their vehicle and drove back to the camp.

Next day, an archaeological party stumbled on the crash site and notified the local sheriff, George Wilcox. Wilcox called the Fire Department. Military personnel, who had been tracking the UFO on radar, also headed for the scene. At the crash scene itself, things were hotting up. Jim Ragsdale and Trudy Truelove had decided to take a second look in daylight and noticed several bodies on the site. They collected up some pieces of the wreckage, but threw them away when they saw the military arrive, fearing that they might be arrested.

Their worries seem to have been well founded. The military took over at once, escorted the archaeologists away and insisted they take an oath of secrecy. Five bodies were taken from the wreckage. Shortly afterwards, the Mortuary Officer at the Roswell Army Air Field phoned local undertaker Glenn Dennis to ask if he had any 1.2-metre-long sealed caskets. He also asked how to handle bodies that had been exposed in the desert. The officer assured Dennis both requests were purely for information.

As it happened, Dennis was not just an undertaker, but an ambulance driver under contract with Army Air Field. Later in the day he was called out to pick up an injured airman and take him to hospital. Three field ambulances were on the scene. In one of them, Dennis saw some very strange wreckage. A nurse told him he had better leave and an officer threatened him with dire consequences if he ever spoke about what he'd seen.

Meanwhile Mac Brazel, the rancher who had heard the explosion in the thunderstorm, went out to inspect his lands and there discovered widely strewn metallic debris that included some very odd metal foil and parchment with floral designs on it. He showed some of it to his neighbours, who suggested he should bring it to the sheriff. Brazel did so the following day and Sheriff Wilcox notified the military. An army intelligence major and a counter-intelligence officer visited Brazel's property, took away two car loads of the debris and

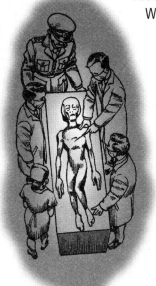

decided to have some of it flown to Washington, D.C., for analysis.

On Monday, July 7, undertaker Dennis asked a nurse from the military base out to lunch. Over the meal she told him she had assisted in an autopsy of several small bodies that had large heads, huge eyes, concave noses and slit mouths. The smell from them was so bad that even experienced doctors had to leave the room. The military then issued a press release stating they had recovered the remains of a flying saucer that had crashed near Roswell. Predictably this created headline news. *The Roswell Daily Record* led with the story **RAAF Captures Flying Saucer on Ranch in Roswell Region**.

But then, as Major Marcel, the Intelligence Officer involved, was on his way to Washington with the debris, he stopped off at Fort Worth. The senior officer on the spot, General Roger Ramey, promptly took charge of the material and ordered a press conference to pronounce that it was nothing more than the remains of a weather balloon. Later, the US Air Force explained that the 'aliens' seen by various witnesses were dummies dropped from a high altitude as part of an experiment in human endurance.

But as the US military continued to insist no extra-terrestrials had crashed in New Mexico, a civilian named George Adamski stepped forward to claim one landed safely in Desert Centre, California.

THREE

CONTACT

George Adamski saw his first UFO on the night of October 9, 1946. He was living on the slopes of Mount Palomar in California and he was a keen amateur astronomer. When news came through of a particularly spectacular meteor shower on that night, he got out his telescope.

As the most intense part of the shower finished, he suddenly spotted a large black object in the sky, cigar shaped and apparently motionless. He assumed it was a new type of aircraft developed during the war and thought it might be studying the meteors at high altitude. Even when it shot off leaving a fiery trail he thought nothing about it. Then he heard a newscast from a San Diego radio station claiming hundreds of witnesses had seen a cigar-shaped UFO hovering over the city. Many of them thought it was an alien spaceship.

On a warm August evening the following year, Adamski was sitting on the swing in his yard when a bright object appeared in the sky above the mountain range to his south. It moved from east to west and was quickly joined by two similar objects. One of them stopped abruptly in mid air and reversed its direction, something impossible for any conventional aircraft of the day. Adamski, who had seen the press publicity about Kenneth Arnold's Mount Rainier sightings, decided he must be watching flying saucers. The experience turned him into a keen saucer spotter and he went on to photograph strange lights in the sky. Then, on November 20, 1952, Adamski hit the jackpot.

He had driven with friends to California's Desert Centre, and then taken the highway to Parker, Arizona. About 17.5 kilometres (11 miles) along this road they stopped the car to look at some volcanic rocks. Adamski wandered off and around 12.30 p.m., his attention was attracted by a flash in the sky. He looked up to see a small saucer-shaped craft drift through a saddle between two mountain peaks to land in a cove just under a kilometre from him. While the lower part of the craft was hidden, a dome on the top remained in sight above the crest. Adamski whipped out his trusted Kodak Box Brownie – a simple snapshot camera – and began to take photographs. Many years later, I was to see the originals of these photos in the collection of Desmond Leslie who co-authored a book about Adamski's experience[1]. They showed a bell-shaped vessel with several spheres sticking from its bottom surface. According to Adamski, it was about 10.5 metres in diameter, made from some sort of 'translucent metal' with portholes and a lens, or possibly a light, on top of the dome-shaped cabin. He believed the spheres underneath were part of the landing gear.

Although he was a firm believer in extra-terrestrial life, Adamski was so taken aback he didn't know what to do next and so did nothing. Then a man appeared at the entrance of a ravine between two hills and gestured to him to come over. Thinking he was a rock

1 *Flying Saucers Have Landed* by Desmond Leslie and George Adamski, Neville Spearman, London, 1970.

collector who needed help, Adamski began to walk towards him. As he got closer, Adamski started to wonder if the man was all he seemed to be. His clothing seemed strange – he was wearing a chocolate-brown ski suit in the middle of the desert – and his hair was very long for the fashion of the day. In every other way, however, he appeared quite normal. He stood just over 1.5 metres in height and was slimly built, probably weighing just under 61 kilograms (10 stone). Adamski estimated he was about 28 years old.

But then the stranger stepped forward until they were little more than an arm's length apart and Adamski was hit by a staggering realisation: "I was in the presence of a man from space – a human being from another world!" He was so stunned he found himself speechless, his mind refusing to function. He felt like a little child in the presence of great wisdom and much love.

The creature greeted Adamski by placing his palms together then began to communicate in a mixture of sign language and telepathy (transmitting of thoughts). He indicated that he came from the planet Venus and was concerned about atomic test explosions on Earth that were affecting the 'environment of space.' He told Adamski that if too many nuclear explosions took place, they would destroy all life on Earth.

Adamski was understandably interested to learn more about the visitor and his culture. The alien told him 'space people' frequently headed Earthwards not only from other planets in the solar system – all of which were inhabited – but from star systems elsewhere in the galaxy. They never landed in populated areas, partly because

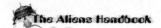

they didn't want to start a panic, partly because they thought they might be torn to pieces. When this curious conversation finished, they both strolled to the spaceship, the Venusian climbed on board and took off.

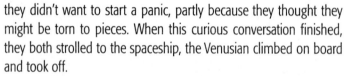

A month later, the saucer was back. Just before leaving on the first visit, the Venusian had asked Adamski for one of his film holders. Now, as Adamski watched, the holder was dropped out of the craft. When he picked it up and had the film developed, it proved to show a rough sketch of a flying saucer surrounded by a series of glyphs (symbols) that might have been some sort of alien writing.

Later still, Adamski's space friends returned again and this time offered him a trip in their craft. Adamski readily agreed and was taken into space on a journey that circled the Moon. He described the far side of the Moon, which had not been photographed at that time, as having an Earth-like environment with forests, rivers and even roads. Even at the time, many people found all this difficult to believe, but while Adamski was arguably the best known of the early saucer contactees, he was by no means the only one. And the others told stories that were just as incredible.

FOUR

CONTACTS SPREAD

In 1953, a Brazilian named Aladino Felix had a brief encounter with a UFO and its crew in the mountains near Paranã, São Paolo. A little later, the pilot turned up on his doorstep to begin the first of a series of meetings during which they discussed astronomy, theology and flying saucer engines. Like Adamski's contact, the alien claimed to be from Venus. Felix went public with the information in a book, published under the pen name Dino Kraspedon, in 1959.

This Venusian seemed able to see the future and helped Felix predict a wave of terrorist attacks in Brazil. The attacks – on police stations and public buildings – subsequently took place, but they were led by Felix himself who was arrested and dragged off protesting that he was the Venusian Ambassador to Earth. He warned that his space friends would invade Earth in order to free him (at time of writing, the invasion hasn't yet started).

Venusian visitors were not, apparently confined to the Americas. Sometime around 1954, a London taxi driver named George King was contacted by an extra-terrestrial voice in his flat. Just over a week later, an Indian swami (holy man) teleported in to teach King how to set up ongoing communications with the alien, a Venusian named Aetherius, who represented an Interplanetary Parliament. King not only did so, but established the Aetherius Society to spread the alien's message.

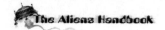

The message contained several unexpected elements, including the information that prayer could be stored in batteries like electricity and that Jesus Christ now lives on Venus. When challenged to prove its claims, the Aetherius Society arranged for a huge spaceship to hover over Los Angeles, but the Interplanetary Parliament rendered it invisible to all but the faithful in order to avoid public panic.

Yet another Venusian entered the life of a South African woman named Elizabeth Klarer. Ms Klarer saw her first UFO as a child in 1917, but contact had to wait until December 1954. Two days after Christmas she spotted a handsome humanoid in a 16.5-metre diameter saucer hovering near her remote farmhouse in the Drakensberg Mountains. Klarer felt frightened, but when the spaceman returned on April 7, 1956, she rushed fearlessly to meet him and was swung laughing into his flying saucer. When he asked if she was afraid, she replied, "I have known your face within my heart all my life."

It was a promising start for a love affair. The spaceman's name was Akon and the result of their passion was a child delivered during a visit to his home planet. Like so many other early contactees, Ms Klarer named that planet as Venus shortly after her initial encounter. But in a 1977 book she contradicted this with the claim that Akon came from the planet Meton in Alpha Centauri, the nearest star system to Earth.

The romantic element of Ms Klarer's experience was duplicated – although with fewer complications – in the case of Truman Bethurum, an American highway maintenance worker. On July 27, 1952, Bethurum was on his break from the night shift and decided to amuse himself by driving into the Nevada desert. He parked near Mormon Mesa and stretched out to take a nap. He awoke to find a 90-metre diameter metallic disc hovering near his truck and ten small olive-skinned men surrounding it.

The creatures, who were about 1.5 metres in height, invited him aboard their craft where he met their captain, Aura Rhanes, a stunningly beautiful woman in a red pleated skirt, a red and black beret and a black velvet bodice. From her he learned that all the planets in our solar system had breathable atmospheres and most of them were inhabited – information that would astonish today's astronomers if they took it seriously.

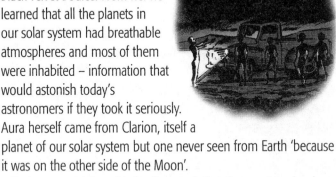

Aura herself came from Clarion, itself a planet of our solar system but one never seen from Earth 'because it was on the other side of the Moon'.

Bethurum and Aura hit it off so well that they met again eleven times over the next three months and swapped information about their respective cultures (life on Clarion was 'simple and harmonious'). Then, just as things were getting interesting, Aura simply stopped coming. Bethurum never saw her again.

Howard Menger was another American whose emotional life became complicated after contact with Venusians. Like Ms Klarer, his first contact was as a child. At the age of 10 (in 1922) he went for a walk in the woods and there met an unusually beautiful woman with golden eyes who not only claimed she came from Venus, but promised Menger her people would contact him many times during his lifetime.

This information turned out to be accurate. Menger received numerous telepathic (thought) messages while serving in the Pacific during World War Two and actually met up with Venusians in various places. The war eventually ended, but the contacts continued. Menger brought the aliens clothing so they could pass unnoticed among humans and in 1956 managed to photograph one of their

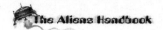
spaceships. In return for his help, Menger was given a piece of extra-terrestrial potato, which contained five times more protein than the Earth vegetable and enabled the extra-terrestrials to live much longer than we do.

Menger's Venusian friends told him that humanoid civilisations were scattered across the entire solar system – something which Menger readily accepted for a curious reason. Both he and his second wife Connie were firmly convinced that they had lived past lives on different planets. Menger was Saturnian, Connie was Venusian, but despite the distance they became lovers. Connie even wrote a book about it in which she identified Menger as a great spiritual teacher from Saturn named Sol da Naro.

Orfeo Angelucci, a worker in the Lockheed aircraft factory at Burbank, California, was also told that he had lived a past life as an alien on another planet. His first contact came on May 24, 1952 when two luminous green globes hovered in front of his parked car and a voice asked him to get out. When he did so, a viewscreen appeared between the globes and the faces of two 'radiantly beautiful' aliens – a man and a woman – appeared to lecture Angelucci telepathically about the fate of our planet and promise further contact.

That contact occurred just two months later when he stumbled on a UFO in a vacant car park. He climbed on board and the craft took off to the sound of 'Fools Rush In' (a popular song at the time) played through hidden speakers. He was again lectured about the fate of the Earth, then bathed in a beam of light that put him in a state of cosmic consciousness. Angelucci landed safely and had further meetings with the aliens. During one of them he was transported spiritually to another planet where a beautiful alien couple told him that he himself had been an extra-terrestrial in a previous life.

The Venusians returned to Britain in 1957 when one of them materialised in the Birmingham home of Mrs Cynthia Appleton. With his one-piece suit and long blond hair, he was almost identical to the creature who visited George Adamski and like that contact and many others, he communicated by telepathy. When Mrs Appleton's visitor came back the following year, accompanied by a friend, she was given the intriguing information that the aliens were not physically present, but appeared as 'projections.' During a later visit one of the beings left behind a small skin sample which, when analysed, gave the appearance of animal tissue.

Despite individual variations, there were several common themes running through the majority of these early contacts. Many of the visitors claimed to be Venusians – at least until astronomers discovered what conditions on Venus were really like. Most were human in appearance, usually extremely handsome with long golden hair and sometimes golden eyes. Contactees often referred to them as 'our brothers from space' and believed them to be wise, spiritual and benevolent. Certainly the space brothers expressed their concern about the spiritual and physical welfare of humanity, urging such sensible courses as the abandonment of nuclear weapons and a more caring attitude towards the environment. Most were 'sweetness and light' – but not all.

In August, 1952, for example, a scoutmaster named Sonny Desvergers was coming back with three boys from a meeting when they noticed strange lights in some woods. Desvergers went to investigate, leaving the boys in his car. When he failed to return, one

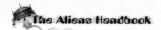

of them sensibly went off to phone the local sheriff. Desvergers stumbled from the woods as the sheriff arrived and told of a terrifying experience. He reached a clearing to find a saucer-like craft floating above him. He shone his torch upwards, a panel opened in the saucer's turret and a creature emerged so frightening in appearance that Desvergers would not even describe it. The creature fired a spray of fiery gas at him, burning the scoutmaster's arms and knocking him out. When he came to, the saucer had vanished.

In September the same year at Flatwoods, Virginia, a group of boys, a local housewife and a young National Guardsman went to investigate what they thought must be a meteor crash. But instead of a meteorite they discovered a huge sphere 'as large as a house' hovering over a remote hilltop. In a nearby tree was a 4.5-metre tall robed creature with bright red skin and glowing greenish-orange eyes. The party fled as the creature moved towards them and some of them were sick because of the stench that came from its body.

Cases like these were the first real hint that the extra-terrestrial visitors might not be quite as harmless as they had appeared. And as the 1950s ended, alien contact took on an increasingly dark aspect.

FIVE

ABDUCTION

An American couple named Betty and Barney Hill were on holiday in Canada in September, 1961 when they heard reports of a hurricane heading towards New Hampshire where they lived. Afraid the storm might cut them off, they decided to make an immediate run for home, even though it would mean driving through the night. Around 9 p.m. on the evening of September 19, they crossed the US-Canadian border and took the US Route 3 highway south. After a stop-off in a restaurant, Barney estimated it would take them a maximum of five hours to get home. He expected to arrive a little before 3 a.m. the next morning.

But shortly after they drove past the village of Lancaster, Betty noticed a bright light in the sky that seemed to be getting closer. At first she thought it must be a star, but it seemed to be following their car. The light stayed with them for several kilometres, appearing and disappearing behind mountains and tree tops. Eventually Barney parked the car and he and Betty walked down the road with their dog, Delsey. The light definitely seemed to be moving. Betty went back to the car for their binoculars and they managed to make out a shape with flashing lights. Barney told her it had to be an aeroplane, or possibly a helicopter.

They went back to their car and drove off slowly. They'd begun to feel very uncomfortable. The aircraft – whatever it was – seemed to

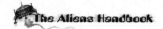

be circling them and they were very much aware they were alone on a lonely road. The UFO came closer. By now they could see it was far too large for a conventional plane, but it was certainly no natural phenomenon – they could make out a double row of windows on the side. Barney continued to insist it had to be a plane, but stopped the car again and got out. He started to walk towards the object, which dropped down to hover about tree-top height. When he was about 50 metres away he suddenly realised there were about a dozen people staring down at him from the windows.

The UFO dropped lower until it was hovering only a short distance above the ground and extended a ladder or ramp. One of the occupants emerged. Barney stood stock still. He was having difficulty looking away from the eyes of the creatures in the craft, which seemed to exert a hypnotic influence over him. Suddenly his paralysis broke. Barney screamed in panic, ran back to the car and drove off shouting that they were, 'going to be captured'. Neither Barney nor Betty could see the strange craft now, but heard a beeping sound at the back of the car and felt momentarily sleepy.

"Now do you believe in flying saucers?" Betty asked.

"Don't be ridiculous!" said Barney. Then came further beeping sounds. The highway was suddenly unfamiliar but they found a road sign, got their bearings and drove directly home without further incident.

It was daylight now. Both their watches had stopped, but clocks in the house showed it was 5 a.m., more than two hours later than Barney had originally anticipated. The couple were exhausted and went directly to bed. They slept until three that afternoon. When they woke, their experience seemed unreal, but when Betty examined their car there were several shiny circles, each about the size of a large coin, burned into the paintwork. Some days later, at the suggestion of her sister, Betty held a compass near them. It spun wildly, showing that the spots were generating a strong magnetic field.

Within a week Betty started to have nightmares about being carried off in a UFO. They got so bad that, much against Barney's better judgement, Betty reported their sighting to the local Air Force Base where details were logged. She also wrote to Major Donald Keyhoe, a former Marine who, since 1957, had been director of the National Investigation Committee on Aerial Phenomena (NICAP).

Although NICAP occasionally investigated UFO reports, the organisation was very wary indeed of anything that sounded like a crank report. It was several weeks before NICAP experts came to interview the Hills, but the couple impressed them. One investigator asked why it had taken them so long to get home on the night in question. Betty and Barney looked at one another. It was only then that they realised how extreme the time difference had been.

Word spread and other experts got involved. Betty was still having nightmares. Barney was uncomfortable discussing his experience. Two suggestions were made to them – that they should retrace the steps of their journey and that hypnosis might help them recall more

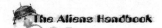

clearly what had happened. The Hills took up the first suggestion almost at once. The experiment triggered no further memories, but when they called at a small restaurant near the town of Woodstock, local residents told them of several UFO sightings in the area. The descriptions of these UFOs – one of which had hovered for almost an hour – sounded identical to the craft they had seen.

It was not until February of 1964 that the Hills took up the second suggestion and then only because Barney suspected that his stomach ulcers might have been made worse by the stress of their experience – and he was worried about Betty's nightmares. He decided to call on the help of Dr Benjamin Simon, a noted Boston neurologist and psychiatrist. Although no believer in flying saucers, Dr Simon was convinced that the couple had suffered a genuine trauma and also thought hypnosis might help recover the lost memories of what really happened. On February 22, 1964, he introduced them to a technique known as hypnotic regression, which takes subjects mentally back in time to remember things they had previously forgotten. Dr Simon regressed both Betty and Barney Hill, meeting with them separately in a series of sessions over a period of six months. The stories they told matched.

Sometime after they saw the UFO on September 19, a group of between eight and 11 small uniformed humanoids with large, strange eyes stepped into the road and stopped their car. The leader told them they would not be harmed and took them on board a disc-shaped aircraft where they were physically examined. Tissue samples of hair, fingernails and skin were taken and a long needle inserted into Betty's abdomen, apparently as some sort of bizarre pregnancy test.

During the two hours they were aboard the strange craft Betty asked the leader where he came from. He showed her a map showing a series of dots connected by broken and unbroken lines. Betty took it to be a star map, with the lines perhaps representing trade routes. She asked which dot was the aliens' home star. The leader, communicating telepathically, asked if she knew where Earth's Sun was on the map. Betty replied that she knew nothing about astronomy and the extra-terrestrial remarked that if she didn't know where she was, there was little point in his showing where he came from.

In the course of the examination, the aliens became intrigued by Barney's false teeth and asked Betty why her teeth were not removable as well. When she told them that some people had to have artificial teeth as they got older, the aliens communicated that they did not understand the concept of ageing since they had no experience of time. Betty and Barney were eventually permitted to return to their car and continue the journey home. The aliens, it seemed, then turned their attention to the abduction of a lot more victims.

SIX

ABDUCTIONS
SPREAD

Five years after the Hill incident, Officer Herbert Schirmer was driving his patrol car on the outskirts of Ashland, Nebraska at 2 a.m. in the morning of December 3, 1967, when he saw the lights of an oncoming truck. Then, as the vehicle came nearer, he discovered the truck was actually a disc-shaped aircraft, which swooped up over his patrol car and disappeared skywards. Schirmer drove back to the police station and wrote up an official record of his sighting. As he checked the time for his report, he realised an hour had somehow gone missing. The following day he fell ill with headaches and nausea. An angry red mark came up on his neck.

Like the Hills, Schirmer underwent hypnotic regression. This time the hypnotist was a University of Wyoming psychologist, Dr Leo Sprinkle, who recorded the following story: As the disc-shaped UFO approached, a blurred object emerged from it and flew towards Schirmer. He tried to draw his gun, but found for some reason he could not. His car engine died abruptly.

The investigators tried to convince Schirmer he was suffering from delusions, but he rejected this idea and got in touch with another hypnotist, Loring Williams. Regressions conducted by Williams produced a much more detailed picture. The 'blurred object' that came out of the UFO formed itself into a group of humanoid aliens who sprayed green gas over Schirmer's police car before pointing some sort of stunning device at him. He lost consciousness only briefly, however, and woke to find one of the aliens touching his neck. Schirmer opened the car door and got out.

One of the aliens asked if he was the 'watchman' over the area. Another pointed to the local power plant and asked if it was the only source of energy humans had. The extra-terrestrials then took Schirmer into their ship. He found himself in a large chamber with seats and instrument panels before being taken on a guided tour of the craft. He was told the aliens originated in another galaxy and had set up secret bases in various terrestrial locations. There was also mention of a 'mother ship'.

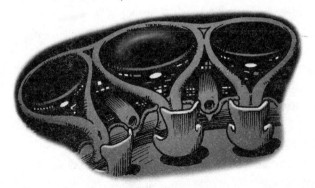

The idea of a mother ship goes back to George Adamski. Various witnesses have claimed sightings of a huge craft, often cigar-shaped, which remains aloft while the smaller, saucer-like vessels explore our planet from close range and sometimes land. Schirmer's aliens added the interesting information that the saucers were sometimes disabled by Earth radar, but were actually destroyed by the mother ships before they could crash – presumably as a way of insuring no wreckage was examined by humans.

After some further conversation, Schirmer was taken back to his

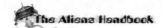

car, told he would remember only the UFO landing, and released. The UFO and its crew then flew off. Schirmer added the intriguing detail that each alien wore an insignia depicting a winged serpent.

Throughout the 1960s, report after report of this type continued to pour in to the Air Force, police authorities, UFO investigation organisations and anybody else who would listen. Over the years a pattern has emerged: the individual concerned is usually alone, often in bed, on a lonely road, or in some isolated rural location. The experience may start with a feeling of unease or the appearance of a light. Memory loss is usual at this point, so that the victims will typically remember the light and sometimes the appearance of a saucer-shaped craft. Then a sort of time slip or blank occurs, so they find they have driven a great distance without any awareness, arrived home without knowing how they got there, or simply woken up in their beds as if nothing untoward had happened.

The memories of what actually did happen during the blank period sometimes emerge spontaneously, sometimes through dreams or nightmares, but can usually be recovered very successfully by means of hypnotic regression. Each experience is unique, but here again abduction investigators have noted the emergence of various typical features. First, there is the arrival of the alien entities. They are most usually (but not always) described as small humanoids – just over 1 metre tall – with spindly limbs and disproportionately large, hairless heads. Except for their eyes, their faces are almost featureless: tiny ears or no ears at all, a tiny nose and a small slit for a mouth. The eyes, by contrast, are huge, almond-shaped and jet black, often without any sign of an iris or pupil.

These creatures usually display extraordinary control over physical matter. They frequently show the ability to pass through solid walls or locked doors, sometimes with the apparent aid of a blue beam of light. Their victims experience immediate and total paralysis before being floated out of their environment – again often through solid walls on the beam of blue light – and into a waiting UFO either parked on the ground or hovering overhead.

Once inside the saucer, a medical examination (of sorts) begins. Although physical force is seldom used, the victims seem powerless to resist. They are undressed, laid out on a table or couch and probed and prodded by the aliens. Tiny metallic devices are often implanted in their bodies, usually by being pushed up the nose. The aliens show considerable interest in human reproduction. They extract ova from female victims, sperm from males. Sometimes they implant embryos in the womb of a human woman or extract foetuses – possibly alien-human hybrids previously implanted – that are already there.

Following on this distasteful aspect of the abduction, victims are then examined very thoroughly using high-tech machinery that often seems to float above them. While this is going on, screens show them pictures that can range from scenes of mass destruction to love scenes, leading some investigators to speculate that the aliens are recording the bodily effects of various emotional responses. If the victim is female, she may be taken into a type of nursery area where she is shown alien-human babies or children – usually fairly sickly – and encouraged to hold or nurse them.

Sometimes the abduction can take on a particularly nasty turn with the victims immersed in tanks of liquid or put in great pain. When the whole thing is finished, they are returned to their normal environment, although not necessarily to the exact spot where they were abducted. Memory loss is almost universal.

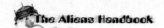

Not all these features are present in every abduction, but it is a rare abduction that does not include at least one of them. And the overall number of abductions has increased at a truly alarming rate since the Betty and Barney Hill case in the early 1960s. A 1991 survey of almost 5,947 Americans indicates that the overall number of abductions at that time ranged from a low of several hundred thousand to a possible high of 3.7 million. And this was only in one country. Elsewhere there were equally dramatic signs of alien activity.

SEVEN

S I G N S

Towards the end of the 1960s, farmers in Australia started to notice curious circular marks in their fields of cereal crops. These were labelled promptly (somewhat jokily) 'saucer nests'. A link between flying saucers and crop circles was quickly established in Britain as well. During the 1960s, the Wiltshire town of Warminster became world famous as a place where UFOs were frequently seen, often in considerable numbers. In May, 1980, a local farmer named John Scull discovered an odd circular mark in a field of oats overlooked by the famous Westbury White Horse – a chalk carving on a high hillside. Mr Scull thought nothing of it, but when he noticed two more on August 13, he talked to the *Wiltshire Times*, which ran a small item about them. The circles were large – 18-and 19-metre diameter respectively – and some 135 metres apart. The bigger of the two circles was decorated by symmetrical outward and inward spurs.

Two UFO experts were on the spot within a day of the report to investigate. They noted there were no tracks leading to the circles and concluded the oats were somehow flattened by air pressure, but made no link with flying saucers. Only a little while afterwards, however, such a link was made in the national news magazine *NOW!*

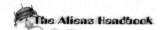

when, like their Australian versions, the circles were referred to as 'landing nests.' Over the next few years, nearly a third of all crop circles were linked to UFO reports.

A year later, more crop circles appeared, this time at Cheesefoot Head, near Winchester. They were rather more spectacular than the first example – three circles in a line, with the middle one substantially larger than the other two. They also looked artificial, rather than some natural phenomenon. All the same, physicist Terence Meaden was quick to suggest the circles were caused by a rare type of whirlwind. The sites of these and the earlier Wiltshire circles had a similar environment and weather conditions were much the same at the time each formation appeared. In August 1982, two more circles turned up, this time at Cley Hill, Warminster, from which crowds had watched out for UFOs since the 1960s.

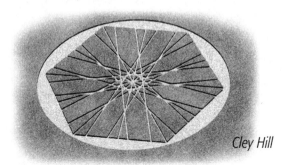

Cley Hill

On July 8, 1983, a spectacular five-circle formation appeared mysteriously at Westbury. Crop circles promptly jumped from a local phenomenon to a countrywide preoccupation. Most of the mass-circulation newspapers played up the possibility of a UFO connection and an American tabloid, *Weekly World News*, claimed a giant saucer had landed in a wheatfield creating problems for the farmers.

Scientists didn't believe it. By now the favourite theories among them were based on the idea of a natural vortex – a sort of minitornado whose swirling winds flattened a portion of the crop – or on microwave radiation generated by equally natural pockets of plasma (electrified air particles). In 1990, however, two circles were discovered connected by a straight line. Clearly swirling winds or swirling plasma could not account for that. It began to look as if some sort of intelligence was behind the phenomenon ... but that had to include the hand of a hoaxer.

In the years that followed, the crop circle phenomenon became more widespread and more complex. Intricate, and often very beautiful, designs began to appear. Something akin to a Tudor Rose motif appeared in a barley field in Hampshire. A spiral of diminishing circles (with symmetrical little out-liers) turned up in a wheat crop near Stonehenge. There was a circle encasing two six-pointed stars in Wiltshire. Another pattern in Essex featured three crescent moons.

Several Wiltshire patterns were spectacular in the extreme and really took the phenomenon well beyond its initial 'circle' description. At Alton Barnes, for example, there was a design that looked like two interwoven strings of threaded pearls. A Liddington wheatfield produced a sun/moon motif. At Iddington, the crop was shaped into something that looked like a giant scorpion. Windmill Hill threw up a spiral design. Another circle enclosed a chequerboard design.

Scientists pointed out the similarity between some crop designs and the beautiful patterns of fractal geometry generated by computers. While not necessarily contributing to the theory of a

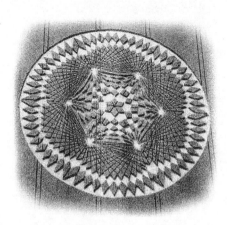

Windmill Hill

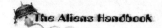

UFO connection, many observers felt the beauty and sheer complexity of the crop patterns completely ruled out most of the proposed natural causes.

Then, in 1991, two 60-year-old Englishmen, Doug Bower and Dave Chorley claimed on national television that the crop circles of Britain were hoaxes and they were the hoaxers. They had, they said, invented the whole idea of crop circles as long ago as the late 1970s and had personally made most of the patterns that had excited public attention since that time. The two hoaxers claimed that from 1978 until 1990, they were responsible for all the simple circles found in Britain. After that they decided to make their work more complicated when the vortex theory was put forward. What's more, they demonstrated before the cameras that using only the simplest equipment – surveyor's tape and a 'crop stomper' made from a length of string and a wooden plank – extraordinarily complex designs could be created.

Following in the wake of Doug and Dave, other hoaxers came forward to grab their moment of 'me-too' fame. It looked as if the mystery of the crop circles had been solved ... and there was no UFO involvement whatsoever. But after the initial flurry of excitement, doubts began to creep in. Examination of early circles had shown seed heads were missing and nodes in the stalks blown out, as if through microwave action – not the sort of effects that follow the use of a simple crop stomper.

Then there was the discovery that some circles caused batteries to go dead, compasses spin wildly and wristwatches change their setting, sometimes while their wearers watched. Crop circles seemed capable of affecting human beings as well with reports of people fainting while in their vicinity. On one farm, the land within two crop circles became sterile: not even weeds would grow on it.

It seemed the mystery was not solved after all. Ufologists and crop circle investigators recalled that Doug and Dave had claimed credit only for British circles that appeared since 1978. But crop circles were a worldwide phenomenon, appearing in the U.S.A., Canada and Russia as well as Britain. Some of them contained plants that had simply fallen over undamaged, clearly not bent and damaged by a stomper. Even more to the point, there were circles reported before 1978 when the jokers claimed they started faking them. In 1975, for example, officials in Minnesota, U.S.A. discovered a total of 47 in a single field. And Doug and Dave themselves freely admitted they'd been inspired by reports of the Australian 'saucer nests' which had not been their work.

Thus the investigation continued after the Doug and Dave confession. In 1991, crop circles were discovered on property owned by the Prince of Wales, who was so intrigued that he asked to be taken on a tour of British crop circles (the arrangements were dropped when the press got wind of them). By August 2000, experienced investigator Colin Andrews concluded approximately 80% of all modern crop circles were man-made – and had infra-red video evidence to back it.

But while some of the remaining 20% might be due to undiscovered hoaxers, investigators have noted electrical fields are definitely associated with the phenomenon – the Earth's natural magnetic field sometimes mirrors the circle design, as iron filings mark out magnetic lines. Investigator Diahann Hughes thinks the cause is a 'higher intelligence'. Many of her colleagues still suspect that this intelligence may drive a flying saucer.

EIGHT

HISTORIES

There was at least one crop circle for which Doug Bower and Dave Chorley never claimed the credit. It was recorded in *The Natural History of Staffordshire*, whose author, Robert Plott, dated its appearance to 1686, more than two centuries before the two jokers were born. The Staffordshire circle was discovered after an eyewitness saw a group of small, lightly built beings dancing round and round in a field.

Crop circles are not the only things to appear earlier than most people imagine. The entire UFO phenomenon – complete with alien contacts and abductions – falls into that category. Kenneth Arnold's 1947 sighting of flying discs was previewed not just by the foo fighters, but by similar discs reported over North Carolina in 1923. These were seen by so many people that there was an official inquiry (it reached no conclusion).

Long before George Adamski saw his cigar-shaped 'mother ship', a luminous cigar-shaped object flew over Huntington, West Virginia, in 1915. A year earlier, on October 10, British observers noted a similar UFO crossing the Sun. And the year before *that* (1913) a similar object, this one equipped with lights, was seen over several parts of South Wales.

On Christmas Eve, 1909, a luminous, saucer-shaped craft was visible for 32 minutes over Limerick, in Ireland. There was a luminous disc as large as the Moon over Vittel, France, in May 1908. On July 2 the previous year, a cigar-shaped UFO hovered over Burlington, Vermont, and witnesses described how a small, luminous disc emerged from the craft and flew off. Three luminous discs, flying in formation at a height of 1,524 metres, were reported by the crew of the SS *Supply* on February 24, 1904.

Powered flight had been developed at this time, but only just. On the morning of December 17, 1903, America's Orville Wright managed 36.5 metres through the air in 12 seconds. By the end of the day, his brother Wilbur flew 260 metres over the sand in 59 seconds. For the first time in history, say our official records, a heavier-than-air machine had achieved powered, sustained flight under the control of a pilot.

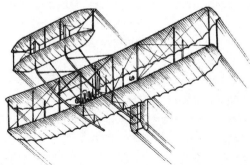

Yet flying discs were twice reported over France in 1899 and again the same year over El Paso, Texas and Prescott, Arizona. Two saucers, flying in close formation, were visible for six minutes over England during the summer of 1898. Two years earlier, a disc flew over Worcester on the night of December 17 giving out so much light that one witness remarked you could have seen well enough to pick up a pin.

Disc-shaped aircraft were reported over Ireland and England in 1895, over Wales in 1894, flying in formation between Shanghai (China) and Japan in 1893, crossing the Moon in 1892, rising out of

the sea near Cape Race (Canada) in 1887, over China in 1885 – where it was visible for eight minutes before disappearing behind a cloud – and over Chile in 1883.

That was the year (1833) when UFOs first got photographed. On August 12, the Mexican astronomer José Bonilla was observing the Sun from Zacatecas Observatory when a procession of 143 UFOs crossed its face.The UFOs appeared again next day and the well-prepared Bonilla took photographs with a newly invented camera attached to his telescope. His prints showed not only discs, but cigar- and spindle-shaped flying objects. In a report of his sightings, he estimated that the objects had passed over the Earth at a height of 321,800 kilometres (200,000 miles).

Between then and 1871, there were UFO reports from Hungary, America, France, Wales, the Persian Gulf, Russia, England, Holland and Belgium. In 1871, a giant disc-shaped UFO hovered over Marseilles in France for nearly ten minutes, then moved north, halted and moved east. It was visible for 20 minutes and described as reddish in colour. Saucers and other UFOs continued to be seen right through the 1860s and back into the 1850s, including a stream of them observed via telescope and reported by the Reverend W. Read in 1851, the year of London's Great Exhibition. This procession of saucers lasted from 9.30 a.m. to 3.30 p.m. On October 26, 1846, a flying disc dropped a 200-kilogram lump of foul-smelling jelly on Lowell, Massachusetts. (Foul-smelling jelly has dropped out of the sky before and since. It is known as *pwtr ser*, which I understand is a Welsh term meaning 'rot of the stars'.)

By this period of history, there was no such thing as powered flight, according to our official records. Henri Giffard of France constructed the first successful airship – driven by steam– in 1852. To carry the engine he had a 44-metre-long hydrogen bag and flew at 9.5 km/h (6 mph) for 32 kilometres (20 miles). The first rigid airship, with a hull of aluminium sheeting, wasn't built until 1897 –

yet in 1826 a grey, cigar-shaped object was seen approaching Earth by observers in France.

There was no manned flight of any sort before 1783, when the first hot-air balloon was designed by the French brothers Joseph-Michel and Jacques-Étienne Montgolfier. Yet UFO reports were commonplace before that date. In 1779, a flight of glowing saucers passed over Boulogne, in France, two years after astronomer Charles Messier reported a large number of discs in the sky. In 1755, bright flying globes were seen over Lisbon in Portugal. (They were back again, in procession across Switzerland, in 1761, and may have been similar to globes seen earlier over Florence, Italy in 1731.) UFOs appeared over England in 1661 and Switzerland in 1619.

But even these early reports fail to tell the full history of the UFO. In 1557, Henriopteri of Basel, Switzerland, published the first edition of Conrad Lycosthenes' *Prodigiorum Ac Ostentorum Chronicon*, a heavily illustrated book depicting various 'prodigies' (in Old English this means 'marvellous things') and monsters. These were considered to be real creatures in the Middle Ages. Page 494 of the work includes a woodcut of what appears to be a spaceship. The text explains it was seen over Arabia in 1479. This rare work is not the only indication of UFOs in Medieval times. Frescoes on the walls of a 14th Century church in the former Yugoslavia show strange aircraft with little men inside. Surviving Medieval prints show the panic caused in European populations by processions of luminous discs in the sky.

But even these are relatively late sightings. In 234 BC., three UFOs were reported in the sky over Rimini, in Italy, the first of many such sightings over the next century or so. These reports, recorded by the Roman historian Pliny, referred to 'flying shields,' and their appearance came to be thought of as an omen (sign or warning). Hannibal's troops were reportedly 'buzzed' by flying discs as they crossed the Alps.

An even earlier civilisation has left us a written record of UFO sightings. The *Royal Annals* of Tuthmoses III, dating back to the 15th Century BC., tells how scribes of the House of Life in Egypt saw a fiery disc about 46 metres in diameter descend from the sky. A few days later, the sighting was repeated, but now the single UFO had become a vast number, witnessed by the Pharaoh and his entire army. Astonishingly, these were not the very earliest accounts. In ancient China, bright discs in the sky were known as 'fiery dragons' and the paths they flew were carefully charted on the ground. Nobody was allowed to build on a 'dragon path' and only the Emperor could be buried beneath one. There are even rock paintings in Africa that look suspiciously like flying saucers, suggesting the phenomenon actually started sometime in the depths of prehistory.

This is borne out by two ancient Indian texts, the *Ramayana* and the *Mahabharata* that describe a prehistoric kingdom called Kurukshetra. Although dismissed as a myth by Western scholars, many Indian academics believe the works tell of a genuine historical tradition. If they are right, it is a tradition that includes flying machines suspiciously like today's flying saucers. In the *Ramayana* we find mention of a 'vast aerial chariot named Pushpaka which, gleaming like a pearl, planed above the highest building'. The aircraft is described as 'gilden and bright as the sun with its seats of emerald and pearl, its rooms ranged about, silvered all over…'. The epic describes a long flight, including landings and take-offs, with the hero Rama describing his aerial viewpoint of various landmarks on a journey from India to Sri Lanka.

A Sanskrit document entitled the *Vymaanika-Shaastra* describes the construction of aircraft in ancient India, the training of pilots, principles similar to radar, plane to plane radio communication and spy devices capable of listening in on enemy aircraft. These ancient craft, named *vimanas* in the texts, seem virtually identical in outward appearance to modern flying saucers.

UFOs, it seems, have been with us always. As, apparently, have alien contacts and even abductions.

NINE

ANCIENT CONTACT

Although inventors had been experimenting with airships since 1852 and even managed a few short flights, there were problems with steering that weren't solved until 1901. All the pioneering work was being done in Europe – mainly in France and Germany – and the longest flight ever achieved (over Switzerland) was less than 800 kilometres (500 miles).

Yet in April 1897, thousands of Americans reported the appearance of 'airships' over towns and farms throughout the United States. More to the point, many of them claimed to have met their pilots. Where did these curious aircraft come from? There is no historical record of anybody making them in the States and not a single vessel then constructed anywhere else was capable of a transatlantic flight. Today, every one of these sightings would have to be classified as a UFO. Meeting their pilots would be seen as a suspected alien contact. The only doubt about labelling these UFOs stems from the fact that there *were* a few airships known to be in existence at the time, even though they were all so far from America that the well-known inventor Thomas Edison hadn't even heard of them. He went on record as saying that he believed airships would be constructed one day, but the current sightings were definitely a hoax.

There are, however, no problems at all with the sighting that occurred near Alençon, France in the summer of 1790 – more than

half a century before the very earliest experimental airship. At about 5 a.m. on the morning of June 12, a group of peasants spotted an enormous globe in the sky that crashed into a hilltop, uprooting bushes and starting grass fires. The peasants alerted the local authorities so that two mayors, a doctor and three other officials quickly arrived on the scene. According to the police report of an inspector dispatched from Paris to investigate, all these responsible men were present when a door of sorts opened in the globe and a humanoid creature in a close-fitting suit appeared. The creature muttered something in an unfamiliar language, then ran into the nearby woods. Moments later the globe abruptly disappeared in a silent flash, leaving only fine powder behind.

Far earlier, in AD 840, the Archbishop of Lyons recorded the crash of a flying vessel with four occupants, three men and a woman, who were promptly stoned to death by farmers. Tragic though it was, the farmers' behaviour has to be seen in the context of a time when any form of flying machine would have been considered supernatural and quite possibly evil. Many French peasants in the Middle Ages firmly believed in the legendary Magonia, a mysterious other-worldly country whose people rode in cloud ships and raided humanity's crops.

Even in 1686, several hundred years later, the appearance of alien

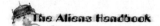

visitors was interpreted as a supernatural event. The eyewitness who watched the little people dancing around the first reported crop circle referred to them as 'fairies'. Contacts with small humanoids – often described as 'fairies' – have been reported throughout northern Europe for centuries. These creatures were believed to abduct humans, who frequently experienced 'missing time'. They were reported to possess 'magical' powers that enabled them to paralyse and 'bewitch' people, so taking control of them. They could change the structure of matter in certain circumstances and ordinary locks seemed incapable of keeping them out. Furthermore, they sometimes married humans to produce curious children, or kidnapped human children to raise as their own. All these activities, along with many descriptions of the fairies themselves, are identical to those reported in relation to UFO aliens in modern times.

This would be peculiar enough if 'little people' were confined to Europe, but they are, in fact, widely reported in Asia and, to a lesser degree in Africa and the Americas. The Tzeltal Indians of Mexico, for example, preserve legends of the *ihk'al*, small humanoids who fly with the aid of rockets strapped to their backs and sometimes abduct people. Other native Mexican peoples tell stories of flying beings who kidnap women and force them to bear children. In Brazil, there are legends of small, winged creatures with telepathic powers. The fairy tradition is not the only hint that alien contact is an ancient phenomenon. The Bible is full of stories about creatures who come from the skies to interfere in the lives of people. They are referred to as God's messengers, or angels.

Like UFO aliens, angels can turn up anywhere and at any time. In the Old Testament when King Nebuchadnezzar attempted to execute Shadrach, Meshach and Abednego by throwing them into a furnace, an angel appeared out of nowhere to ensure they were unharmed. The King remarked that the angel was like the son of God. Sons of God are first mentioned in *Genesis* where they are described as mating with human women to produce remarkable children. A much fuller account of this appears in the *Book of Enoch*, where they are referred to as 'angels' or 'children of the heaven.' Several writers on ancient history have suggested the story reads more like an account of extra-terrestrial visitors than a religious myth. American researcher John A. Keel has pointed out that there is a similarity between many 'angel' names, such as Uriel, and those of the creatures contacted in UFO encounters.

Certainly the angels described in the Bible – and in particular the Old Testament – are not always the kindly, powerful supernatural beings of modern mythology. They are described as eating and drinking, capable of committing murder and of being beaten in a fight. But if stories of fairies and angels (perhaps with the addition of meetings with demons) really do represent an interpretation of the modern 'close encounter' phenomenon, then it would appear aliens have been around our planet – and interfering in human affairs – for thousands of years.

Just how many thousands may be judged from Tassili rock carvings in the Sahara Desert which seem to show a humanoid space traveller making contact with an ancient civilisation. The carvings have been dated to around 6000 BC, more than 8,000 years ago.

The Theories

PART TWO

TEN

NOTHING HAPPENING

So what's happening here exactly? According to the government and military authorities in most countries … absolutely nothing. In 1947, the US government undertook a preliminary study of flying saucer reports, which concluded among other things that the phenomenon was real and the discs appeared to be as large as man-made aircraft. A recommendation was made that a fuller study should be undertaken. This resulted in the establishment of a full-scale investigation, code-named Project Sign, at the end of December.

The following year, Project Sign produced a top secret estimate of the situation that concluded the UFOs were probably interplanetary vessels. When the document reached Air Force Chief of Staff, General Hoyt S. Vandenberg, he ordered it destroyed on the grounds that the evidence did not support the conclusion. Project Sign was replaced by Project Grudge in 1949. This new (or possibly just renamed) project adopted two interlinked policies. The first was to explain away every possible report as the result of misunderstood aircraft, balloon, meteor etc sightings. The second was to investigate witnesses rather than their reports with a view to questioning their mental state.

Then, just two years after Arnold saw his UFOs, Project Grudge underwent another name change, this time to Project Blue Book. But the basic attitudes remained the same. All Project Blue Book did was collect and record flying saucer reports. The Air Force was curious, but not *very* curious and certainly far from alarmed. The sightings were viewed at this time as a mixture of hoaxes, mistakes and hallucinations. There was nothing up there that couldn't be explained; and probably nothing up there at all.

But then something happened to set off alarm bells. In July, 1952, witnesses reported strange craft in the skies near the Washington National Airport. At the same time, air traffic controllers recorded the UFOs on their radar screens. It was the first ever radar confirmation that the saucers weren't just tricks of the light, distant planets or hallucinations. That worried the authorities. Clearly there was something solid in the skies over Washington – and it was far too near the National Airport.

Nobody wanted to start a panic. It was only 14 years since America's Mercury Players broadcast a radio programme based on H.G. Wells' novel *War of the Worlds*. The play was broadcast like a real news report. When the announcement was made of an attack on New Jersey by invaders from Mars, thousands of listeners took it seriously and ran screaming into the streets. It wasn't difficult to imagine what might happen if the public discovered there might be *real* aliens about to land.

So instead of releasing the news, the US Government quietly shifted the emphasis of Project Blue Book by setting up another investigation briefed to do little more than simply collect case histories. The panel was headed by a professor of physics from the California Institute of Technology and included meteorologists, engineers, physicists and one astronomer. It was set up under the direction of the CIA (Central Intelligence Agency). Panel members found they now had high security clearance and were briefed about various military activities and intelligence the public knew nothing about, but which might – just might – have had a bearing on the saucer sightings. They were also told their findings would be classified *Secret*.

The number of reported UFO sightings continued to increase after 1952. Perhaps more importantly, reports started to come in from outside the United States. There were, it seemed, saucers flying over Britain, Europe, the old Soviet Union, Australia and Asia. With such a volume of material pouring in, a second Blue Book panel was set up in February 1966. Like the first, it was told to keep its findings secret. But to the embarrassment of the authorities, some respected scientists began to air their thoughts publicly around this time. UFO investigators like the astronomer J. Allen Hynek and the meteorologist James E. McDonald put forward the theory that a small percentage of the most reliable saucer reports pointed towards the presence of extra-terrestrial visitors.

The idea produced massive excitement. To try to stem it, the US Air Force set up yet another UFO study in 1968. This one was led by the physicist Dr Edward U. Condon and called on the services of no fewer than 37 scientists. They investigated a total of 59 UFO sightings and concluded early in 1969 that the extra-terrestrial theory was nonsense and no further investigation was needed. The American Government took this to heart and closed down Project Blue Book a little later in the same year.

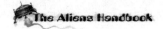

In its published conclusions, Project Blue Book claimed that after 19 years of investigation, nearly 95% of all reported UFO sightings could be accounted for by things like bright planets, meteors, ion clouds, aircraft, birds, balloons, searchlights or pockets of hot gas, sometimes complicated by unusual weather or atmospheric conditions. The experts indicated that none of the 12,618 reported UFOs had 'ever given any indication of a threat to national security.' This last conclusion was a lie. On October 5, 1960, when Project Blue Book was already 11 years old, what appeared to be a missile formation was picked up by American early-warning radar at Thule in north-west Greenland.

At this time, the Cold War between America and the former Soviet Union was at its height. Each side was deeply suspicious of the other. Both were convinced that a nuclear missile attack might be launched at any minute. To meet the threat, America had established a worldwide grid of radar stations designed to alert the military well in advance of the rockets reaching American soil. Once an attack was confirmed, it was American policy to launch its own massive nuclear strike deep into the heart of the Soviet Union, so beginning a war that would leave the world a nuclear wasteland. The policy became known as Mutually Assured Destruction, or MAD for short.

As technicians charted the course of the incoming missiles, they discovered the blips on their screens had come from somewhere over the Soviet Union. It was quickly confirmed that they were heading directly for the United States. A sombre official picked up the red telephone and placed a call to Strategic Air Command Headquarters in Omaha, Nebraska. US forces worldwide went onto an immediate Code Red nuclear alert. Fighter planes were scrambled in every military airfield. A-bomber B-52s, already in the air as part of the country's standing nuclear deterrent, were given their preliminary codes. It only required one more signal to start a worldwide nuclear war.

Strategic Air Command demanded urgent confirmation that the incoming missiles were what they seemed to be. Worryingly, the generals found all lines of communication with Thule had suddenly gone dead. It seemed the early-warning station had already been destroyed. But there was no doubt at all about the existence of the missiles. US ground radar was now picking them up. The military could wait no longer. They placed an urgent phone call to the President, briefed him on the situation and asked for orders. The world teetered on the brink. Then the 'missiles' suddenly changed course and disappeared. The global nuclear alert gradually wound down. Later investigation showed communications with Thule had been cut by an iceberg. The 'missiles' were a UFO formation.

Incidents like this were not the only reason why so many people – including scientists and other experts – declined to accept the, 'Nothing to worry about, folks' conclusions of Dr Condon. Even if the Blue Book figures were accurate, the 5% (more accurately 5.6%) of unexplained sightings accounted for more than 700 cases over the life of the project.

Project Blue Book was the last example of open US Government involvement with flying saucers, but official records of sightings continued to be kept in Canada, Britain, Sweden, Denmark, Australia and Greece.

At time of writing, none of these countries has issued any official explanation for the flying saucers. All maintain a sceptical (disbelieving) public attitude towards the phenomenon. Scepticism towards contact reports is even more pronounced. but to be fair to the governments concerned, it's a scepticism that's widely shared.

ELEVEN

LIARS AND LUNATICS

ven as a young UFO hunter, you may have noticed a few problems with those early reports of contacts with flying saucer crew. George Adamski's account, in Chapter Three, shows many of the difficulties. Let's go back to the first encounter. A spaceship lands and out steps an alien creature in a zipperless ski suit and size 9 shoes who looks just like you or I – except prettier, according to Adamski, who claimed the beauty of its form went beyond anything he had ever seen. This creature breathes our atmosphere without any difficulty.

Already Adamski's announcement is beginning to sound suspicious. An ability to survive on an alien planet without a spacesuit, or at least a helmet, isn't quite an impossibility, but it's so unlikely that it starts you asking serious questions. The most obvious is – .how could a humanoid life-form develop on Venus?

When Adamski met his visitor, Venus was something of a mystery planet. Astronomers knew it was approximately the same size as the Earth – it was often referred to as our 'sister planet' – but its surface was frustratingly hidden by cloud cover. This led scientists to think that there might be life beneath the clouds, possibly even intelligent life. In Adamski's day, a man on Venus was a real possibility.

But it isn't a possibility any longer. Unmanned probes have shown that Venus has an atmosphere of 96% carbon dioxide and a surface temperature of 460°C, hot enough to melt lead. Those clouds aren't water vapour – they're concentrated sulphuric acid. The surface is a barren wilderness of basalt (black rock formed from lava), broken up by active volcanoes. No water, no vegetation, no people, no spaceports.

Perhaps Adamski misunderstood his visitor – they were, after all, communicating through a mixture of sign language and telepathy – but his description of the far side of the Moon leaves a lot to be desired. Once again science has caught up with guesswork. Our own spacecraft have now circled the Moon and taken photographs of its hidden side ... which looks very much like its visible side. No forests, no lakes, no roads, no signs of life at all.

Although both Venus and the far side of the Moon were unknown in the early 1950s, another detail of Adamski's supposed space trip was met with disbelief even at the time. He claimed to have seen fireflies when he glanced through one of the saucer's windows. Everybody knew a firefly could not survive beyond Earth's atmosphere. So, after an initial flurry of excitement – his book *Flying Saucers Have Landed* became a bestseller – science caught up with Adamski and he was lumped together with history's other cranks, lunatics or fakes.

Most of the early contactees went the same way. A majority of them insisted that many, if not all, the planets in our solar system supported humanoid civilisations. Then, when science showed this was impossible, the stories were quietly changed to place the alien visitors in other galaxies. It seemed clear that those who claimed to have met space brothers were in it for the money (Adamski wasn't the only one to produce best-selling books), for the fame (1950s contactees attracted considerable press attention), for the followers (people like George King established what seemed to be flying saucer religions) or simply because their minds were seriously disturbed. But was it really that clear?

Although most of Adamski's reported experiences read like bad science fiction, there are one or two details of his accounts that raise uncomfortable questions. For example, the alien he met in the desert told Adamski of radiation belts encircling the Earth. Adamski remarked in his book that he was particularly sure of this information (conveyed by sign language) because his Venusian used the heat radiation from the desert floor as an example.

There really are two radiation belts encircling our planet, doughnut-shaped zones of high energy particles trapped in the Earth's magnetic field. But they were not discovered by American physicist James A. Van Allen until 1958 – several years after Adamski reported their existence. Nor is there any possibility that Adamski discovered the belts himself as part of his amateur astronomical observations. Van Allen needed data transmitted by the US *Explorer* satellite to establish their existence.

If this was the only piece of accurate information collected by Adamski, we might write it off as coincidence. But there are other aspects of his accounts that stand up to examination. Those 'fireflies' he mentioned seeing through the window of his flying saucer seem to have some basis in reality. John H. Glenn, the first US astronaut to circle the Earth in 1962, reported an unexpected electrical phenomenon surrounding his craft that gave the appearance of fireflies. How did Adamski know?

And how did he know about a curious glow of light beyond the stratosphere confirmed by astronauts L. Gordon Cooper, Jr. on the last flight of the Mercury programme in 1963 and Walter Marty Schirra, Jr., command pilot of the *Gemini 6* mission which made the first rendezvous in space in 1965.

Even his nonsensical description of the far side of the Moon might actually reflect something you could expect to see from the window of a flying saucer. On January 7, 1969, the popular French magazine *Paris Match* published a series of aerial photographs that seemed to have been taken over Central Europe. The photographs showed what appeared to be green forests divided by a mountain range and a great river. There was even a clearly defined road system. But this was not Central Europe or any other earthly location. The photographs were taken by the crew of *Apollo 8* as their spacecraft orbited the Moon. Their appearance was the result of an optical illusion, but one that would certainly have fooled a naïve observer like Adamski.

Then too, almost all Adamski's critics ignore the fact that he was not alone when he met his 'Venusian'. There were six people with him, all of whom signed documents swearing they had also seen the craft and its pilot. Only one of the six, George Hunt Williamson, followed Adamski's example in writing books on UFOs and related subjects. The rest seem to have got little from giving their evidence except public ridicule. In January, 1955, four of the six abruptly

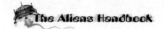

contradicted themselves to claim they had *not* seen anything Adamski reported. The remaining two stuck to their original stories.

As a UFO hunter, you'll find many – perhaps even most – contact reports riddled with these apparent contradictions: items of unexpected accuracy mixed with absolute nonsense, claims, counter-claims and denials. You'll need a clear head to keep track of the information and a particularly open mind to decide what's really useful and what is not.

But even if you decide not all UFO sightings and contact reports are the work of liars and lunatics, there are still a great many other possibilities for you to choose from. One of the most popular is examined in the next chapter.

TWELVE

THEY CAME FROM OUTER SPACE

Before the their bosses ordered them to think differently, Air Force experts at Project Sign concluded that the flying saucers most likely flew in from another planet. In 1947, that sounded like a sensible suggestion. There are nine planets in our solar system – Mercury, Venus, Earth, Mars, Jupiter, Saturn, Uranus, Neptune and Pluto. You can see eight of them with a good pair of binoculars. The one you can't see is Pluto, which needs a proper telescope.

Three conditions are important for the development of carbon-based life (the only sort we know about) on any of those planets – temperature, water, and atmosphere. Although you don't have to have exactly the same temperature range, volume of water or

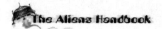

atmosphere as you have on Earth, scientists set limits beyond which life simply can't exist. These limits are bounded by what they call an *ecosphere*.

The ecosphere of our Sun runs from Venus to Mars. One planet within that ecosphere (Earth) is known to have abundant life. In the days before space probes and the Hubble telescope, the other two planets were believed to be real possibilities for life as well. Venus's cloud cover suggested it must have water. And it was just far enough away from the Sun to make sure any people there wouldn't be roasted.

Mars looked even more promising. As long ago as 1844, a French astronomer observed seasonal brightness changes on its surface and concluded they were due to vegetation. Observations of lines on Mars' surface convinced astronomers like America's Percival Lowell that intelligent inhabitants had constructed a planet-wide irrigation system, tapping water from the polar ice caps. But however promising both planets looked in 1947, they no longer look promising today. Although in 1996 NASA (National Aeronautics and Space Administration) announced evidence for ancient microscopic life on Mars, no scientist today believes either Mars or Venus could possibly support intelligent life of any sort, let alone civilisations capable of space flight.

In the light of various findings, most serious UFO investigators have also dropped the idea that the saucers come from any other planet within our system. But some suspect they may have flown in from Outer Space. The belief that there is life beyond the solar system is based on the sheer size of the universe. There are billions of stars in our galaxy and billions of galaxies in the universe. Even if only a tiny percentage of the stars have orbiting planets, the probability of life evolving elsewhere is so high that it is almost certain.

Astronomer Frank Drake created a formula – known as the Green Bank Formula – that attempts to calculate how much of that life is sufficiently intelligent to produce an advanced technical civilisation. The formula is expressed as $N = R*f_p n_e f_l f_i f_c L$ where N stands for the number of technical civilisations in the Milky Way, currently an unknown quantity. The factors on the other side of the equation suggest that to find the number of civilisations you multiply:

* the rate at which stars form ($R*$)

* by the number of stars with planets (f_p)

* the average number of planets per star capable of supporting life (n_e)

* the fraction of those planets which actually develop life (f_l)

* the fraction of those on which the life is intelligent (f_i)

* the fraction of these that get around to building technical civilisations (f_c)

* the average lifetime of such civilisations (L).

Some of the values assigned to those variables are still very much guesswork and different values obviously produce different results. But planets beyond our solar system have been discovered and there is very good reason to suppose the average rate of star formation in our galaxy should be set at 10. In these circumstances, the results of the Green Bank Formula today places the *minimum* number of technical civilisations in our galaxy at 1,000. Some scientists think it could run as high as 100 million.

But even if there *are* 100 million space-faring civilisations in the galaxy, you have to ask yourself why any of them would want to visit us. Earth is a smallish planet circling a mediocre star perched on the edge of a very unremarkable galaxy. There seems little to attract aliens here, even if they knew life had developed. Certainly the reasons that drove men to explore the more distant corners of our own planet does not apply to space travel. Founding colonies makes no sense, nor does trade, nor, despite the best efforts of Hollywood to persuade you differently, does war. The economics of an interstellar voyage are all against them.

Many – perhaps even most – scientists remain sceptical about visitors from space *as a matter of principle*. The problem is the distances between the stars, so great that they are measured in light years, each one representing some 9,437,904,000,000 kilometres (5,865,696,000,000 miles). The nearest star system in our galaxy is Alpha Centauri, which is 4.3 light years away. Astronomers have no reason to believe this system is inhabited. In 1996, they did discover a planet that in theory is capable of supporting life. It orbits the star 70 Virginis, which is 50 light years away.

In the early years of the 20th Century, the great physicist Albert Einstein discovered that it was impossible to accelerate any body beyond the speed of light. The problem is that as your spaceship speeds up, it increases in mass while the flow of time slows. At the speed of light – 299,274 kilometres (186,000 miles) a second – the mass of your ship becomes infinite and time stops altogether, making any further acceleration not merely impossible, but absurd.

With this absolute limit in place, voyages around the galaxy for any alien race would take not just hundreds of years, but thousands – quite impossible within the life span of any species we know of. Admittedly, any species we know of is adapted to Earth conditions and the idea of extremely long-lived alien life-forms cannot be ruled out. But the time element is not the only problem with trips between the stars.

In 1961, the Nobel prize-winning physicist Edward Purcell wrote a special report for the Atomic Energy Commission. In this he worked out the energy that was needed to power spacecraft that could travel at a worthwhile fraction of the speed of light. The figure was so enormous he concluded no civilisation, however advanced, could

12

possibly afford it. The idea, he said, belonged on the back of cereal boxes.

But while the odds seem stacked against the possibility of inter-stellar travel, it may fall into the same category as the old convictions that iron ships won't float and you could never get a heavier-than-air craft off the ground. Both beliefs were perfectly sensible in their day, but took no account of possible technical advances. When you decide whether or not something is *really* impossible, you have to remember that no one thought that iron ships could float or heavier-than-air craft could get off the ground. There is a difference between what isn't possible (yet) because we simply haven't figured how to do it – a *technical* impossibility – and what isn't possible (ever) because it contradicts the laws of physics – an *absolute* impossibility. And when you decide something contradicts the laws of physics, you need to be certain you understand those laws correctly.

Take, for example, the science-fiction idea of faster-than-light travel, which would solve many of the problems of inter-stellar trips. You might imagine that this FTL drive would be a non-starter because it contradicts the laws of physics. Didn't Einstein prove nothing could travel faster than the speed of light? Well, no, actually he didn't. He proved you couldn't accelerate something until it went faster than the speed of light, which is a different statement. Some physicists have thought about the existence of particles (called tachyons) that just naturally travel faster than the speed of light. Since you don't have to *accelerate* them from sub-light speeds, they don't contradict the law Einstein discovered.

So is the idea of a faster-than-light tachyon-powered spaceship an impossibility? It's certainly a *technical* impossibility since we have not the slightest idea how to build one (or how to jump aboard once it's going). But it's not an *absolute* impossibility, which means that a really advanced civilisation somewhere in the galaxy might be able to build and use one. Even Dr Purcell's energy calculations, which

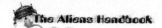

showed that pushing a craft close to the speed of light would need near-infinite amounts of energy, seem less impossible now than they did in 1961. What has changed is the discovery of zero-point energy, a vast reservoir of potential power that exists in the very fabric of empty space. We can't tap zero-point energy yet, but that doesn't mean it's necessarily beyond the reach of a more advanced civilisation.

Other discoveries allow for some very clever ways to get around the light-speed barrier. We now know, for example, that space isn't simply the absence of matter, but a thing in itself which distorts in the presence of a gravitational field. That means if you applied enough gravity, you could bend space. If you applied it cleverly enough, you could fold it up in such a way that a distant star becomes a whole lot closer. As long as space stays folded, you could reach that star in a fraction of the time you would normally need. That way you never travel faster than light, but reach your destination as if you had.

At the moment, the only thing we know that will distort space in this useful way is a stellar mass several times the size of our Sun, hardly the most practical engine to stuff inside a spaceship. But stellar masses several times the size of our Sun have a habit of collapsing into Black Holes, which produce just as much gravity, but may be a little more manageable. (Physicists are now trying to create little Black Holes in their laboratories.) Another possible approach to inter-stellar travel relies on the even more recent discovery that an area of space can contain less than nothing. Quantum physics, the most up-to-date theory of the Universe we have, has shown that the figure which denotes the quantity of energy per given unit of space can fall below zero. In other words, space can contain negative energy. Just thinking about *negative* energy and its solid counterpart, exotic matter, is enough to fry your brains. But physicists assure us these discoveries open up some very exciting possibilities, including a warp drive (a technology that warps space allowing you to travel faster than the speed of light) and a wormhole that could act as a short tunnel through the very fabric of space to a distant location.

Warp drives and usable wormholes are technically impossible at the moment, but certainly not absolutely impossible as a future development. They are probably not impossible at all to an astronomer like Frank Drake, who believes advanced civilisations exist elsewhere in the galaxy. So the UFOs *could* come from a distant star system, despite earlier scientific doubts.

But just because they could, doesn't necessarily mean they do. Even with the transport problems solved, there are still enough problems with the extra-terrestrial theory to persuade Ufologists to look for other explanations of the strange things seen so often in our skies.

THIRTEEN

ALL IN THE MIND

Towards the end of the 1950s, the great Swiss psychologist Carl Jung instructed his secretary to start collecting anything she could find on flying saucers. She went to work and soon had an archive of books, photographs and cuttings that filled several bookshelves and six large box files. Jung, then in his eighties, began to analyse the material. The result was a book, published just two years before his death, entitled *Flying Saucers: A Modern Myth of Things Seen in the Sky*. In it, Jung put forward a very different theory on what UFOs were all about.

Throughout his long life, Jung had been fascinated by the depths of the human mind. He accepted Sigmund Freud's (another famous psychologist) theory of the subconscious – an area of your mind that stores forgotten memories and hidden emotions – but believed this was only a very small part of a much larger mental picture. Jung was convinced he had found evidence for what he called a *collective unconscious*, a large area of hidden mindspace that was the same in every member of the human race.

It was the collective unconscious that produced humanity's great myths, heroic (and sometimes religious) stories which appear in every culture of the world. Myths, he believed, were never literally true, but were always useful in that they taught people truths about human needs and behaviour. According to Jung, myths and the collective unconscious itself contained symbols, patterns and living energies he called *archetypes*. One of the most important archetypes was the mandala, or circle, which appears in Oriental religions as a symbol of unity and wholeness.

Jung felt the shape of the flying saucer – a circle or disc – was very significant in any explanation of what was going on. Writing as he did at the height of the Cold War when humanity was split into two opposing military camps, he believed there was a widespread longing for unity. This longing, he thought, would naturally express itself in projection of the mandala symbol in the form of a flying circle or disc. For many people, Jung seemed to be saying that flying saucers were some sort of collective hallucination, brought on by the stresses of the Cold War. In other words, they were all in the imagination.

But it turned out that Jung didn't believe this at all. He was well aware that UFOs showed up on radar and left actual traces on the ground, which meant there was something solid up there. This puzzled him just as much as it did everybody else. He was at pains to stress that his theory only put forward a possible *reason* for the sightings, not an explanation of what they actually were. When that proved difficult for people to understand, he explained that the saucers might be real objects that simply provided an *opportunity* for mythic projections. Jung's ideas were not well received by UFO investigators, most of whom held firmly to the notion that the saucers came from Outer Space. But then, ten years after Jung's book was published, a French-American astronomer named Jacques Vallée stepped in.

During the early 1960s, Vallée published two books of his own, both of them firmly supporting the Outer Space idea. Then, in 1969, he had a public change of heart. His new book, called *Passport to Magonia*, expanded dramatically on Jung's basic ideas and presented a whole new theory of what UFOs really were. If you've been reading this handbook carefully, you'll recall from Chapter Nine that Magonia was a mysterious otherworld believed in by Medieval French peasants. In *Passport to Magonia*, Vallée compared modern UFO contact reports with folklore that described meetings with supernatural beings. He came to the conclusion that the basic details of each were identical.

This led him to believe that the same phenomenon had presented itself to humanity for centuries and the only real difference was how it was interpreted. If you were a Medieval peasant abducted by a small grey humanoid with huge eyes, you'd tell people you'd been 'taken by the fairies' or possibly tormented by some demon. If it happened to you today, you'd tell everybody you were grabbed by aliens from Outer Space.

In later books, Vallée expanded this by suggesting that the cause of the whole UFO phenomenon was a powerful non-human intelligence set on guiding the spiritual development of our race. Other investigators weren't so sure. Two influential authors, Jerome Clark and Loren Coleman, accepted that the ancients may have seen goblins where we see spacemen, but thought the visions were the mind's attempt to bring a little emotion into the picture to escape from the modern-day emphasis on dry, logical thought. As it happened, both Clark and Coleman later dropped their idea that the saucers were all in the mind because of the evidence that had puzzled Carl Jung when he first put forward his mythic theory – the plain fact that saucers left physical traces.

This would seem to rule out the mental origins of UFOs altogether, were it not for an extraordinary report that emerged out of Tibet before the Chinese invasion of 1950. Its author was a distinguished

French traveller and scholar named Alexandra David-Neel. Madame David-Neel first entered Tibet in 1916, but returned so often and came to know the country's customs and religion so well that she was made a Lama (a priest of Tibetan Buddhism) – the only European woman ever to be honoured in this way. One of the most fascinating things she came across in her travels was the Tibetan belief in *tulpas*.

This belief was that intense visualisation and concentration could make a mental picture visible. Some Tibetans went as far as to say the image could take on a life of its own and behave in many ways like a ghost. It all seemed rather fanciful to Madame David-Neel until she experienced it for herself. She was camped high in the Himalayas when a young painter she knew entered the camp. The man had a special devotion to a particular Tibetan god, which he had painted many times and visualised in the course of his meditations. To her astonishment, Madame David-Neel saw the ghostly – but perfectly visible – figure of the god looming behind him.

She was so intrigued by the experience that she decided to see if she could create a tulpa of her own. The figure she visualised was a plump little monk, rather like Friar Tuck in the Robin Hood legends. It proved hard going: the sort of visualisation recommended by her lama friends was both detailed and prolonged. But eventually she got the hang of it and was able to produce a vivid mental picture of her monk. This was, however, only the beginning. She next had to visualise the monk as if he were actually present – so

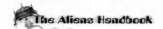

purposely producing a hallucination. That proved more difficult still, but again in time she managed it.

Over a period of several weeks, Madame David-Neel continued to visualise the monk moving around her camp until others finally began to ask who the stranger was – they had started to see the little monk as well. It seemed Madame David-Neel had succeeded in creating a genuine tulpa, a thought-form visible to others. In a cautionary note to her report, she described developments that would do justice to a horror movie. Having succeeded in her experiment, she planned to move on to other things, but the monk began to turn up in the camp even when she had not visualised him. Worse still, he steadily lost weight and his cheerful expression was replaced with a sly, sinister look.

Madame David-Neel realised her tulpa was slipping out of her control and had no idea what to do about it. She took advice and was told it would have to be 'reabsorbed.' It had come from her mind and she now had to draw it back in there again. This turned out to be a lot more difficult than it sounded and it took her months of hard concentration before the monk finally disappeared.

That Tibetan tulpa lore goes far beyond the creation of ghost-like figures, is shown by a very curious spiritual practice involving something called a Yidam. In Tibetan Buddhism, a Yidam is a (rather fierce) god specifically devoted to teaching … and certain Himalayan gurus (teachers) used the Yidam image to teach a very powerful lesson indeed. What broadly would happen was this – a guru would teach his pupil as much as he could, but with a particularly promising pupil the time would come when the pupil started outpacing his teacher. At this point, the guru would suggest he make contact with a Yidam.

To this end, the pupil had to find a lonely cave high up in the Himalayas and there construct a sort of magic circle called a kylkhor. This was a complex operation which took weeks, or even months, to complete, but it was very necessary since a Yidam was a dangerous creature and the kylkhor was needed to restrain it. Once the guru had inspected the finished kylkhor and pronounced he was satisfied with it, the pupil would be instructed to meditate on the Yidam and visualise it strongly as appearing within the magic circle. He was allowed to use illustrations from various scriptures as an aid.

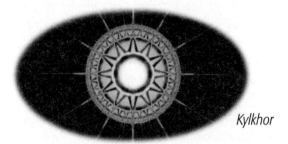

Kylkhor

Clearly the process of concentration and visualisation was identical to that of producing the tulpa. But when the pupil finally reported he could see the Yidam in the kylkhor, the guru would tell him this was not enough. What he had to do now was imagine he could hear the Yidam's voice – and do this so vividly that he could actually hear the words as if the creature were physically present. This part of the exercise would not be considered complete until the pupil could actually carry on conversations with the Yidam.

Once the pupil reported success, the guru would encourage him to go even further and bend his mind to visualising the Yidam so powerfully that he could feel the creature's hands on his forehead in a blessing. Even this did not complete the process. The pupil was eventually instructed to persuade the Yidam to leave the kylkhor circle and accompany him wherever he went. By this point, of course, what began as a thought-form had developed into something the pupil could see, hear and touch, exactly as if it were physically present.

Tibetan spiritual practice did not distinguish between such

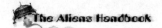

creations of the mind and what we would think of as reality. (In fact, the whole purpose of the Yidam technique was to teach star pupils that the world itself was an illusion.) It was firmly believed that a fully constructed tulpa was as solid as a boulder and quite capable of directly influencing physical matter.

All this seems a long way from the problem of modern UFOs, but in fact it is not. Just after I started on the present chapter, I received a letter from a Canadian researcher enclosing details of a UFO sighting he'd had several years ago. Far from interpreting it as an illusion or a spaceship, he referred to it as a tulpa and was convinced it was something real, but essentially created within his mind.

The linking of Tibetan tulpa doctrines with saucer sightings connects with Jung's ideas about the projection of mythic contents by the collective unconscious. If the Tibetans are correct about their tulpas, the saucers can be both mental and physical at the same time.

But even that has not proved to be the wildest idea about the nature of UFOs.

FOURTEEN

TIME TRAVELLERS

In 1974, an American physicist named Frank Tipler published an article in *Physical Review* under the strange title 'Rotating Cylinders and the Possibility of Global Causality Violation.' Readers quickly discovered that a 'global causality violation' was a very, very weird piece of geometry: a path that wound through space and turned around in time. Tipler called it a 'closed time-like line' and announced that he'd figured out how to make one. Dr Tipler's idea was to build a machine that distorted both space and time. He was even able to explain how to do so in a single sentence, 'Relativity suggests that if we construct a sufficiently large rotating cylinder, we create a time machine'.

Relativity, in this context, was the Theory of Relativity published by the great physicist Albert Einstein in 1905. It showed that space and time weren't separate as everybody thought, but were just pieces of something bigger – the spacetime continuum. And the spacetime continuum could be bent by gravity – the sort of gravity you'd generate if, as Dr Tipler said, you built a big enough rotating cylinder. The sort of cylinder you need would actually have to be huge – far too big to build on Earth. It would be so long you wouldn't have the room to lay it widthways across the whole east-west sweep of the United States. It would also be heavy, far heavier than lead, for

example, or anything else you've ever tried to lift.

What you would need would be a super-dense material, the sort that has enormous mass, but takes up very little room. There's nothing like it on Earth, but as Dr Tipler pointed out in his article, we know this sort of matter definitely exists. Neutron stars are full of it. In fact, neutron stars are *made* of it.

Neutron stars are stars that collapse under their own weight, but don't go all the way to becoming a Black Hole. The electrons inside their atoms smash into the nucleus where they fuse with protons to become neutrons (hence the name). As a result of this, the atoms themselves join together so that the whole star becomes one great atomic nucleus. It's the densest substance in the universe. If you could mine enough of it to fill a teaspoon and fly that teaspoon back to Earth, your payload would weigh more than one million tonnes (and that doesn't include the weight of the spoon!).

But even at that tonnage, a teaspoonful would be nothing like enough to create a Tipler cylinder. Another American physicist, Fred Alan Wolf, estimated that the device would need to be about 40 kilometres (25 miles) across and more than 4,000 kilometres (2,485 miles) long. Making something that size takes about a hundred neutron stars. Once you learn that, it's clear that building a Tipler cylinder would be far beyond our present technology. But that's only a *technical* impossibility. The best theory we have says a Tipler time machine would work in principle. Most scientists agree that if something is possible in theory, technology will learn how to do it sooner or later.

But there was something about Frank Tipler's machine that is really exciting. We know we can't build a Tipler cylinder today, but if humanity learns to build one in a thousand years time, or ten thousand years time, or even a billion years time, the gates it will open will extend throughout the entire spacetime continuum. That means if a Tipler Cylinder is ever built by humanity or an alien race at any time in the future, then somewhere in space, beyond the solar system astronauts will be time travelling.

This is an interesting idea, but perhaps even more interesting is the calculation that the safest, most efficient design for any spacecraft that wished to use the Tipler mode of time travel would be … a flying disc. But the theory that UFOs may come from our future does not depend on the manufacture of a Tipler cylinder, it arises out of the nature of alien contacts. First, while some monstrous forms have been reported, the vast majority have been humanoid, like the small 'Greys' with spindly limbs, large heads and huge nocturnal eyes, or just like humans, as in Adamski's famous 'Venusian.'

We know that every living creature, from a microbe to a milkman, evolves in response to its environment. That's why fish have gills that enable them to breathe water, while you have lungs that enable you to breathe air. It's possible that there's another planet within travelling distance where conditions are so Earth-like that human or near-human forms would evolve, but the chances are against it.

Saucer visitors seem completely at home on our planet. They are not crushed by its gravity. They are not blinded by the Sun. They survive breathing oxygen. This last point is particularly important. Earth is an oxygen-rich environment. Both air and water are full of it. Yet oxygen is a toxic, corrosive gas: it's what causes iron to rust, for example. You and I make good use of it only because we've evolved on this planet for millions of years. A visitor from a truly alien environment would be poisoned by our air and water within minutes.

Another factor that needs to be considered is the many abductee reports which suggest the aliens are involved in a cross-breeding programme with humans. Successful inter-breeding requires genes to match. As the astronomer Carl Sagan once remarked, there is more chance of an elephant successfully mating with a mimosa (a type of flowering plant) than there is of a creature from another planet producing offspring with a human.

Given these facts, some Ufologists argue that it makes far more sense for the saucers to come from a future planet Earth than from some other area of the galaxy. In such a case, many of the creatures encountered would be our distant descendants, perhaps slightly changed in appearance by millions of years of evolution, but still essentially human. Yet you have to ask if there is anything apart from disc-shaped craft to suggest that time travel may one day become possible. Surprisingly, the answer is yes. There is much evidence across the globe that our planet has had visitors from a distant future. It seems some things will never change: time tourists have left litter.

As a UFO hunter, you can spot such litter by asking yourself a simple question: Does the thing you're looking at fit the time period in which it was dropped?

Somebody once dropped several hundred metal balls in South Africa. For years, miners in the Western Transvaal have been finding them in a layer of Precambrian sediment (the Precambrian era was 2,800 million years ago, long before there was anybody about to manufacture metal balls). There are two types – a simple solid metal sphere, bluish in colour with flecks of white, and a hollow orb with a white spongy centre. Many are about the size of a cricket ball. Both are so hard they can't be scratched by steel. All look as if they have been manufactured in some industrial process. But their discovery in Precambrian sediment means they were dropped 2,800 million years ago.

The same goes for the 52 metres of polished concrete block wall found in the depths of an Oklahoma coal mine and estimated to be 286 million years old. Also the delicate gold chain of similar age found in Illinois, the carved stone found in Iowa that was dropped some 260 million years before humanity evolved on the planet, and many, many more, including a decorated metal vase from Massachusetts more than 600 million years old.

In the April, 1862 edition of *The Geologist*, Maximilien Melleville, Vice President of the *Société Académique* of Laon, France, reported the discovery of a perfectly formed chalk ball in an Early Eocene lignite bed near his home. The ball and its immediate surroundings showed evidence of having been carefully shaped from a larger block, then freed by a sharp blow – in other words, it was man-made. There is no question of its having been placed in the stratum at a later date. Melleville was quoted as saying:

> *It ... is penetrated over four fifths of its height by a black bituminous colour ... which is evidently due to contact with the lignite... As to the rock in which it was found, I can affirm that it ... presents no trace whatsoever of any ancient exploitation. The roof of the quarry [where the ball was found] was equally intact in this place and one could see there neither fissure nor any other cavity by which we might suppose this ball could have dropped down from above.*

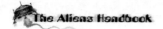

Here again it would seem we are looking at a manufactured artefact, but the placing of the ball puts it an age between 45 and 55 million years, well before the appearance of humanity on the planet. There are a very limited number of explanations for finds of this type. One obvious possibility is that they are simply misdated. But it's difficult to see how you can misdate something like the Massachusetts vase that was actually discovered encased in solid rock.

Another possibility is that the artefacts were dropped not by human time travellers, but by visitors from space. This seems a little more reasonable except that many of the artefacts are of human origin. The carved stone from Iowa, for example, featured multiple representations of an old man's face. There was a fossilised human shoe print (with an embedded trilobite fossil) found in Utah shale some 500 million years old. A human footprint was discovered in the

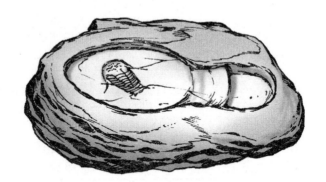

Turkmen Republic of Eastern Europe, next to that of a three-toed dinosaur.

The dinosaurs disappeared from our planet, quite suddenly, some 65 million years ago. Until that happened, the most advanced mammal on the face of the globe was a little tree-dweller no larger than a mouse. Modern humanity itself is supposed to have evolved in Africa no longer than 100,000 years ago – and while there may be a case for adjusting this date backwards, nobody suggests we could have walked the Earth in the days of the dinosaurs. Unless, of course, we travelled back in time.

For some UFO investigators, the time travellers who walked with dinosaurs are the same creatures who cause much excitement when their vessels appear on our radar screens today. But others, it has to be said, are not so sure.

FIFTEEN

THE NAZI CONNECTION

Occam's Razor is a principle which insists you are never allowed to offer an unlikely or complicated explanation for a mystery when a simple, likely one would fit the facts just as well. Some UFO investigators apply this principle to reject ideas like time travel or visitors from space as fanciful. To them, the most likely explanation of the UFOs is that they come from the here-and-now of planet Earth and always have done. They believe the discs are made by all too human hands.

This theory points to the fact that virtually every major country in the world has its own development programme for advanced weapons systems and aircraft design. Such programmes are normally kept secret, as are the results of their experiments. Some are so secret their very existence is denied by the authorities.

In the light of these facts, it makes sense to assume that any disc-shaped craft appearing in our skies is most likely to be part of a secret weapons programme. The theory also goes a long way to explain why the authorities have made such efforts to explain away flying saucer sightings as meteors, weather balloons or the planet Venus.

The theory is strengthened by the knowledge that prototypes (first basic models) of disc-shaped aircraft *have* been produced by one or two manufacturers. There is even movie footage that shows one – dating back to the 1950s – making an attempted take-off. It was not an impressive sight, but it is reasonable to argue that the designs may well have been improved by now.

Some Ufologists have put forward a variation on this basic idea. They claim the saucers were originally of German origin and are still being manufactured in a top secret Nazi base hidden beneath the ice sheets of Antarctica.

According to this theory, the first such craft was designed in 1942 by Flight Captain Rudolf Schriever, a serving officer in the *Luftwaffe*. He called it his 'flying top' and produced a working model powered by a small gas-turbine engine. German Air Ministry officials saw the model fly under remote control and were so impressed they authorised the development of a full-sized version capable of carrying a pilot and small crew.

The 'flying top' became the *Flugelrad*, or 'flying wheel,' just one of various names under which the Nazis were to develop disc-shaped craft. Shriever himself oversaw two major disc projects, one of which was sited at Peenemünde, where German scientists worked on a highly successful rocket programme. Following British air raids that destroyed the test site in August, 1943, the project was moved elsewhere. By summer of the following year, Schriever was in occupied Prague, improving on his earlier designs by replacing the old gas turbine engines with an advanced form of jet propulsion.

At this stage, discs were being built with a diameter of more than 40 metres and were capable of reaching speeds of 2,011 km/h (1,250 mph) at an altitude of over 12,000 metres. When it became clear in 1945 that Germany was going to lose the war, Schriever destroyed his prototypes to prevent their falling into Allied hands, but the story of the German flying discs did not end there.

Years before, in 1938, underwater mapping experts who formed part of a Nazi expeditionary force to Antarctica discovered an enormous deep-water trench running underneath the continent. Two years later, the Nazis established a full-scale scientific and military base – code-named Base 211 – in vast underground ice caverns with its only access through the trench.

In 1945, with their country collapsing around them, top German scientists and engineers were evacuated to Base 211 and there continued to develop their flying disc technology. This development proved so successful that the Nazis were able to repulse a US attack (kept secret by the Americans) and later trade old examples of their technology to both America and the Soviet Union who embarked on saucer programmes of their own. These programmes, and Base 211 itself, combine to explain the various saucer sightings over the years.

Whether or not this fanciful story is actually true, the idea that UFOs are both official and top secret is supported by an incident that occurred in 1952, following a saucer sighting in Italy. The witness, Carlo Rossi, told no one of what he'd seen, but was nonetheless approached by a man in a dark suit who quizzed him about the encounter and gave him a cigarette that made him feel dizzy and nauseous. This incident was the first of many in which men in black have approached witnesses of UFO events – including alien contacts – and warned them not to discuss their experiences with anyone.

The men in black usually claim to be with the FBI, the CIA, some unnamed secret Government organisation or, less often, a UFO investigation organisation. They drive large, expensive (if usually old-fashioned) cars with fake number plates. The reason for their activities seems to be to keep UFO sightings under wraps – exactly what you would expect if the saucers were part of some top secret government project.

As against that, many investigators are convinced there is evidence that the men in black are not at all what they claim to be. They point to cases like that of Herbert Hopkins, who was visited by a man in black on September 11, 1976. At the time, Dr Hopkins – who lives in Maine – was investigating a UFO encounter reported by a man named David Stephens.

While alone in his home, Dr Hopkins had a phone call from somebody in the New Jersey UFO Research Organisation (a group that doesn't exist) asking if he might come over to discuss the Stephens case. Immediately Hopkins agreed, he saw a man approaching his home. The visitor was entirely dressed in black, but as Hopkins showed him in he noticed his visitor was completely hairless – no eyelashes, no eyebrows, no hair on his head.

What followed was like something out of a B-movie. The man in black sat perfectly still and asked questions in a monotone. At one point he asked Hopkins to take a coin from his pocket, hold it in the palm of his hand and watch it. Hopkins did so and the coin dematerialised before his eyes. "Neither you nor anyone else on this planet will ever see that coin again," the man in black promised. He then went on to say that Barney Hill (the abductee mentioned in Chapter Five) had died because his heart had disappeared just as the coin had done and demanded

Dr Hopkins destroy all his records in the Stephens case. During the conversation, the man in black drew a gloved hand across his face and smeared lipstick he was wearing. As he did so, Dr Hopkins realised to his horror that his visitor actually had no lips at all, beyond those drawn on with the lipstick.

The conversation ended with the man

in black speaking more and more slowly until he said, "My energy is running low…must go now…" He walked out unsteadily and Dr Hopkins watched him turn a corner of the house, at which point there was a bright flash of blue light. Hopkins ran to see what had happened, but the man in black had vanished. Incidents like this have led investigators not only to question the MIB's claim to be official agents, but wonder whether they are even human.

Like Dr Hopkins' visitor, they all seem to have a threatening air about them, while at the same time few, if any, contactees seem to think of confronting them directly or asking them to leave. This has led to the belief that they may use a subtle form of mind control. Another odd fact is that MIB behaviour, speech and dress seem curiously old-fashioned as if they originated in the 1940s or 1950s, or have imitated characters in old movies.

All this has led some Ufologists to think that far from being investigators or government agents, men in black are actually part of the whole UFO/alien phenomenon. And as such, they originate not from space, but from a whole different reality.

SIXTEEN

ALIEN DIMENSIONS

ack in the 1930s, some physicists with nothing bettter to do decided to find out what would happen if they fired sub-atomic particles[1] at a screen with two slits in it. They set up a particle generator, which you can think of as a gun that shoots a spray of tiny cannonballs. They set up a screen with two slits they could open and close when they wanted to. And they set up a target that automatically recorded the number of hits by cannonballs that got through the slits. Then they started the gun firing. Common sense would tell you that if they closed both slits, no cannonballs would hit the target. Which turned out to be exactly what happened.

Common sense would also tell you that if you opened two slits in the screen, twice as many cannonballs would get through than if you only opened one. But when they actually tried it, that didn't happen at all. *More* little cannonballs got through with one slit open than with two. The thing about sub-atomic particles is that you can't see them, even with a microscope: they're so small that light actually knocks them aside. You can only try to guess what they look like by studying how they behave.

16

---

1 At one time scientists thought the smallest possible bit of solid matter was an atom. But when the atom was split, they discovered even smaller things inside it – sub-atomic particles.

Up to this point, physicists had always thought of sub-atomic particles as little cannonballs. But since they clearly weren't behaving like little cannonballs, somebody suggested maybe they were actually little waves. Waves would solve the mystery of the double slit experiment. A wave would go through both slits at the same time and since waves sometimes cancel each other out, you'd expect fewer to get through with both slits open than you would with only one.

The trouble was, close examination showed that while particles certainly behaved like waves when they were passing through the slits, they went back to behaving like little cannonballs when they hit the target. Why did this happen? There are two main schools of thought among physicists and you're not going to believe either of them.

One is that the particle begins as a little cannonball, but as it approaches the screen there's a probability of its going through one slit or the other. That probability acts as a wave (a probability wave) effectively splitting the universe in two while it goes through both slits simultaneously. Then, since somebody – usually the physicist – is watching what happens in the experiment, the act of observation causes the probability wave to collapse and the particle to return to being a little cannonball.

Got that? Thought not. Einstein hated it too, although it's the theory a majority of quantum physicists (scientists who study the smallest particles in the universe) accept today. He said he couldn't believe the entire universe would change just because a mouse looked at it. But fortunately there's another theory to explain the same set of facts. A sizeable minority of physicists think the real explanation doesn't involve waves at all. They believe the little cannonball really does go through both slits at the same time. But since this is impossible in a single universe, there has to be another, parallel, universe where the ball goes through the second slit. And since you can have more than two slits in the screen, there has to be a whole series of parallel universes to accommodate the particles.

Whatever Einstein thought about mice looking at the universe, his own Theories of Relativity supported the idea of parallel universes. The maths not only accurately predicted the existence of Black Holes, but showed that they are gateways to an infinite number of alternative realities.

The British astronomer Fred Hoyle took up this idea and ran with it. He suggested that you and I wander in and out of parallel universes (without even knowing it) throughout our lives. Since they're very close they're very similar, but the one we happen to be in determines which slit the cannonball goes through. Not that it matters, of course, because there are parallel versions of you inhabiting many of the parallel worlds. Somewhere in this multiverse you're a famous pop singer. Somewhere else you're dead.

Some Ufologists claim that in some of these parallel worlds there are little humanoids with large heads and huge eyes who've found a way of crossing into this one. Interestingly, this is a very old idea indeed. The ancient Vedic texts of India describe our universe as just part of several realities, all of which are inhabited by various animal and vegetable species, many intelligent and some close to humanity in appearance. Certain of these species are kindly disposed towards mankind, others very hostile.

These texts contain some claims of considerable interest to a UFO hunter. First of all, many of the Vedic aliens are described as living on other planets, complete with their own environments and vegetation. Although these aliens are clearly close as a heartbeat – they seem literally capable of reaching human reality with a single step – their worlds are often described as far away.

This strange situation is resolved in modern astrophysics which recognises that if we could pass through a Black Hole (which we can't) there is the possibility of reaching not just an alternative reality,

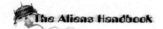

but a different – and distant – part of *this* reality. What we are talking about here are holes in space, which indicate that a planet existing light years distant could be no more than a walk away if we understood the fabric of reality a little better and had the technology to exploit it.

Some saucer-hunters have speculated that what the Indian texts describe is identical to the modern UFO phenomenon, but interpreted in a different way. This is supported not only by ancient descriptions of god-like beings who look suspiciously like Adamski's 'Venusian', and demons who remind you of the small, large-eyed 'aliens,' but also by the fact that the intruders are often associated with 'flying chariots' similar to today's flying saucers. The texts list actual numbers of intelligent species in contact with humanity. The contactees' reports that the 'space people' are interested in the spiritual welfare of humanity also mirrors the religious nature of the Indian texts.

If the Vedas really *do* contain descriptions of UFOs and alien contact, then we have to admit the possibility that the people of Ancient India actually knew more about the phenomenon than we do today.

PART THREE

The Investigation

SEVENTEEN

DETECTING
FLYING SAUCERS

Okay, now you've learned the history of UFOs, complete with alien contact and abductions. You've also learned the major theories that try to explain them. What you have to do now is put all that out of your head and start to investigate the whole thing for yourself. What you discover may lead you to believe one of the existing theories, or it might encourage you to dream up a new one for yourself. Either way, you'll be better placed to make your mind up about one of the strangest mysteries facing the world today.

But how do you go about investigating flying saucers? Your first – and most obvious – step is to see if you can spot one. That means watching the sky. Which sounds so obvious you'd think it was hardly worth mentioning, but the fact is all of us can go for days, weeks, even months at a time without giving the sky more than a passing glance.

So, as you go about your daily routine, develop a habit of looking up as much as possible. Or rather, as much as *safely* possible – you won't do much saucer-spotting if you've just walked under a bus. Not all flying saucer sightings occur at night – Kenneth Arnold saw his in broad daylight – but in most countries the majority of them do, so you need to keep an eye on the night sky as well. That means two things. The first is actually getting out there and watching it.

Leave aside a regular hour or two each week, more if you can manage (make sure your folks are OK about this). Obviously clear nights are better than cloudy, but remember that you're watching for UFOs not stars. Partial cloud or high cloud won't stop you seeing them if they happen to be flying low.

The second thing is to learn a bit about the night sky you watch regularly. You've already read that government officials like to tell flying saucer spotters they've actually been watching the planet Venus. I hate to say this, but those government officials are often right: people who aren't familiar with the night sky *can* confuse Venus – which is a very bright object low on the horizon – with a UFO.

Venus isn't the only thing you need to know about, of course. Get yourself a beginner's guide to astronomy from your library and take time to read up on the sort of thing you might expect to see in the night sky normally. You'll find a number of things that *could* be mistaken for UFOs. Here are some of them, along with a little advice on how to avoid mistakes.

The Night Sky...

Stars

You have to be pretty dumb to confuse a star with a flying saucer, but it does happen. The big difference is that stars don't move in relation to each other. Flying saucers can hover, but if you watch one long enough it will usually move, or disappear. The only thing that will make a star disappear is a passing cloud or dawn. Stars also twinkle, flying saucers don't.

Planets

Planets don't twinkle and they do move in relation to the fixed stars – the ancients called them 'wanderers.' But they move very slowly when compared to UFOs and they follow a clearly defined path in the sky. Your astronomy book will give you an idea of where to find each visible planet in the sky and the path it takes across the zodiac on any given date. Once you have this information, your chances of mistaking one for a saucer drop to zero.

Meteors

These are more tricky. Hundreds, sometimes thousands, of meteors pass across the sky every night, so your chances of seeing one are actually quite high. They're bright, they move fast, they can disappear abruptly and they don't follow a fixed path. It's possible that a genuine flying saucer could be mistaken for a meteor and one or two probably are, but meteors don't stop, hover, change course or reverse themselves – all common flying saucer characteristics.

Comets

Visible comets are rare and attract a lot of media attention, so the chances are you'll know if one is scheduled to appear in the night sky. But assuming you never watch the news or read a paper, you can tell the difference between a comet and a saucer fairly easily. Comets typically move very slowly across the sky, taking days, weeks or longer to move out of sight. You'll track a saucer for an hour or two at most. More to the point, comets have tails (they were once called 'hairy stars') which isn't a saucer characteristic that I've ever heard of.

Aircraft

Night-flying aircraft are obliged by law to show lights which are sometimes mistaken for UFOs. You'll find these lights blink regularly, while the typical saucer appears as a steady light in the sky. Once again, planes tend to follow a steady course, moving much more slowly and less erratically than saucers. Finally, if you take off the personal stereo you will usually be able to hear the aircraft engine.

The Day Sky...

The Sun

You'd imagine it would be absolutely impossible to confuse the Sun with a flying saucer, but there are those who would argue that it's happened – and happened big time. When crowds of several hundred turned up to witness the reported religious visions at Fatima in Portugal, many claimed that the Sun moved about in the sky. Some Ufologists reckon that some apparent meetings with Our Lady and other religious figures are actually part of the whole UFO phenomenon. If this is true, then the 'moving Sun' at Fatima could have been a highly luminous, low-flying saucer that blocked out the real Sun.

Comets

On a really close pass, comets can become visible in daytime. See the info in the Night Sky section for ways to tell them apart from saucers.

Ball lightning

Ball lightning is a rare phenomenon – so rare it's only recently that scientists have come to accept it exists at all. It seems to be composed of luminous, electrified gas and the size of the sphere can vary from that of a cricket ball to a beach ball. A small lightning ball close by can easily look like a large object at a distance. Unfortunately, ball lightning behaves exactly like a real flying saucer – it can move quickly, change course abruptly, hover, reverse itself and disappear. To tell the difference between the two, your best bet is to be very cautious about flying saucers that appear in a thunderstorm.

Weather balloons

Ah, the famous weather balloons! But let's face it, weather balloons do get sent up from time to time and if you've ever seen one, you have to admit they can look a lot like a flying saucer: they're often metallic in their colouring and can give a high-tech appearance from a distance. If you happen to glimpse one briefly out of a plane window, you could easily be fooled. All the same, it's not that difficult to tell a weather balloon from the ground. Apart from gaining altitude, a balloon can only go where the prevailing wind takes it, so like several other things seen in the sky, it doesn't usually move like a flying saucer. That said, a weather balloon can abruptly change course as it moves from one strata of wind to another, so you do need to be careful.

Aircraft

You'd think it wouldn't be hard to tell an aeroplane from a flying saucer in broad daylight, but you'd be wrong. On two occasions I watched a low-flying silver disc transform itself eventually into a winged commercial airliner. On both occasions, the plane was heading towards me at an angle lit from the side by a Sun that was low in the sky.

The combination was enough to produce a striking optical illusion that must have caught out many more UFO spotters than myself. If it happens to you, the trick is to keep watching before you rush off to file your report. Given enough time – and in one of my two cases 'enough' was nearly three-quarters of an hour – the angle of light or, more likely, the angle of the plane will change enough to break the illusion.

Kites

They make them in all shapes and sizes, but to be honest while one might fool you for a minute if seen from a distance, it's quite hard to confuse a kite with a flying saucer if you take the trouble to watch it carefully. Look out for the trailing string.

Radio-controlled powered balloons

The trouble with these big boy's toys is that they're actually *designed* to look like flying saucers (and at least one type is sold as a flying saucer). They consist of a disc-shaped reflective silver-coloured balloon driven by a small, radio-controlled motor. You can buy huge versions more than 2 metres in diameter and I very badly want one. Get the hang of the controls, fly the saucer through the tree tops at dusk and you're guaranteed to start the biggest flap since the *War of the Worlds* was broadcast telling Americans the Martians were coming. These craft can move in any direction and hover just like the real thing, but they can't come anywhere near matching actual saucer speed and manoeuvrability. The other thing to note is that you have to see one fairly close for it to look like a saucer and that really should be close enough for you to notice you're actually watching a fake.

Lenticular clouds

Most cloud cover looks about as much like a flying saucer as a plate of egg and chips, but lenticular formations are a definite exception. These are long, stretched-out clouds that can – and do – sometimes shape themselves into spectacular pseudo-saucers, which can even look silver in the right lighting conditions. I've seen photographs where you'd swear you were looking at the real thing. But the illusion only works in still photographs. If you're watching lenticular clouds, you'll notice they don't move and as you get closer, it becomes more and more obvious what they actually are.

While it's good to know what's up there, the fact remains that even if you learn to tell the difference between real saucers and flying rubbish, you can't watch the sky all the time. Wouldn't it be great if somebody invented a device that would warn you whenever there was a flying saucer in the area? That way you could go about your business and only rush out to scan the sky when there was a real chance of seeing something interesting.

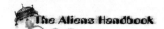

Let me tell you a story. In my days as a magazine editor, I went to interview the 'Dean of Saucery', Desmond Leslie, co-author with George Adamski of *Flying Saucers Have Landed* and acknowledged expert on all things UFO. It was an interview I approached with some fear. Desmond had only recently punched out the journalist Bernard Levin on national TV (because Levin had given a bad review to a performance by Desmond's actress wife) and I was worried he might do the same to me if I happened to ask a difficult question.

My worries increased when Desmond opened the door of his flat – he was the biggest man I'd ever seen; well over 2 metres tall. But as it happened, we hit it off brilliantly. The interview went well, but throughout the afternoon I was intrigued by a little black box in the middle of the floor attached to a snaking maze of electrical wiring. "What's that?" I asked before I left.

"That's a flying saucer detector," Desmond said. "It buzzes if there's a flying saucer in the area."

I thought he was pulling my leg (Desmond had a weird sense of humour) but it turned out the black box was exactly what he said it was. Engineers interested in UFOs noticed that contact reports very frequently mentioned electrical failures in the vicinity of a flying saucer. Lights went out, radios ceased to function, cars stopped and so on. Since this was clearly an electromagnetic field phenomenon – the field generated by the saucer interferes with electrical apparatus – they decided to build a machine that would detect fluctuations in local electrical current. It was a detector of this sort that Desmond had on his floor.

Unfortunately, these early detectors were not particularly reliable – you can have fluctuations in local current for all sorts of reasons that have nothing to do with UFOs. But since then, devices have been invented that sense any large metallic object flying overhead or, in some cases, sense electrical fields of the type believed to be generated by flying saucers.

Even these are less than 100% effective: a large metallic flying object could be a conventional aeroplane, for example. But they certainly alert you to the possibility that there's *something* worth looking out for and that can put you a step ahead of your fellow UFO hunters. You can buy a stylishly designed detector at **www.ufo-detector.com** for $98.50. If that's a bit steep for your budget, they come in kit form at $39.95. Another useful website, **www.futurehorizons.net/ufo.htm** will sell you plans only for $20.

EIGHTEEN

A NATURAL HISTORY OF THE ALIEN

To watch the movies you'd think there was only one type of alien – little spindly-limbed creatures with big heads and big eyes, usually referred to as 'Greys.' Unless you've been skipping pages, you'll know from this handbook that's not the case, since one or two other alien types have already been mentioned. But one or two doesn't cover the whole subject. Since the day Kenneth Arnold spotted his flying discs skipping across the sky, you would hardly believe the number of different alien types that have been reported at one time or another. Even the Greys aren't all alike: some are bigger than others, some have different skin colouring or texture, some have more or fewer fingers.

Dr Thomas Bullard, of the University of Indiana in the U.S.A., analysed abduction reports to try to find out what was going on and came up with three broad classifications of alien – the human, which look, sound and act just like you or me; the humanoid, which look much the way humans do (two arms, two legs, a body and a head) but display noticeable differences; and the non-humanoid, which generally look like nothing you've ever seen before.

This is a start, but it doesn't go anywhere nearly far enough, especially when you get to the non-humanoid group which lumps together creatures that clearly have nothing to do with one another

other than the fact that they don't look human. You can see the problem if you imagined yourself categorising the animal kingdom that way – giraffes, bats and bluebottles would all be considered much the same thing, simply because none of them looked much like your mother.

Brazil's Jader U. Pereira tried to get around this with the logical classification of aliens into just two categories – those able to breath air and those who can't. It seemed sensible enough until you looked at the results … and found you were right back to the giraffe-bat-bluebottle syndrome. There seem to be dozens of totally different alien species able to cope with our atmosphere; and dozens of totally diverse alien species who aren't. To try to improve his classifications, Pereira added in categories based on things like clothing, hair length and the use of tools. Unfortunately these aren't really species differences. Your hair is a lot longer than mine (especially since I shaved mine off) but that doesn't mean we belong to a different species.

An American researcher named Patrick Huyghe made a good effort at sorting reported encounters into four classes, Humanoid, Animalian, Robotic and Exotic, each of which he then subdivided into types. The result was as follows:

CLASSES:	Humanoid	Animalian	Robotic	Exotic
TYPES:	• Humans • Short Greys • Short Non-Greys • Giants • Non-classics	• Hairy Mammalian • Reptilian • Amphibian • Insectoid • Avian	• Metallic • Fleshy	• Physical • Apparitional

Huyghe went on to add variations of each type to produce one of the most comprehensive listings we have. You can use the Huyghe table or create one of your own, but either way you won't get very far until you know what the various types look like. Since decent photographs of aliens are very difficult to get hold of, here are a few artists' impressions of the more common types. Use them as guidance when you start your career as a UFO hunter and add drawings of your own once you begin to gather reports.

Classic Grey

The head is large in proportion to the body, which is usually no bigger than that of a 5-year-old child, with spindly arms and legs. The eyes are large, dark, almond-shaped and slanted. The nose is almost non-existent and the mouth is tiny. Various Greys have been reported as having between three and six fingers.

Classic Human

This type seemed to be almost the norm in the early 1950s and still appears from time to time today. Typically seen wearing a one-piece silver suit, the human type is often described as strikingly beautiful and witnesses are sometimes unable to decide whether they are male or female. They vary somewhat in size and facial characteristics, but by and large any of these aliens would easily pass for human at one of your parents' drinks parties.

Humanoid

Strictly speaking, anything with two arms, two legs, a body and a head has to be classified as humanoid, but what we're really talking about here is something nearly human, but not quite. The creature might have Vulcan ears, peculiar eyes, a blue skin or whatever, so you'd never really assume you were talking to the boy next door.

Reptilian

The big thing here is usually the scaly skin. Reptilians may be generally humanoid (arms, legs, body, head) in appearance, or they may not. The head and/or neck may be elongated and some have been reported to have scaly tails. Clawed feet or hands are not all that uncommon either. One theory holds that many people in positions of authority, including the British Queen and members of the Royal Family, have been taken over by reptilian aliens who work hard to maintain the original human appearance.

Insectoid

Again often roughly humanoid in form, this type is characterised by its enormous and sometimes multi-faceted eyes, which are even larger than those of a Classic Grey and tend to be rounder in shape. The body, whatever form it takes, tends to be slight, with brittle, spindly limbs. Hive behaviour – i.e. lack of individuality – is sometimes reported in connection with Insectoid aliens, but to be fair, this sort of behaviour is often associated with Greys as well.

Hairy Mammalian

If you think of the Tibetan Yeti, or North American Sasquatch (Big Foot) you have a fair idea of what the Hairy Mammalian type of alien looks like. The creature can, and usually does, look more animal than human, despite its basically humanoid shape. Size varies quite considerably from a little over 1.75 metres to nearly 2.5 metres. In contrast with many other alien species, this type tends to have a powerfully muscular build.

Metallic Robot

Robots in our culture tend to be mechanical arms put to work on automobile assembly lines. By contrast, robotic aliens are usually humanoid in shape but clearly mechanical and often metallic (but see 'Fleshy Robot' below). In the 1950s, many robot aliens were reported as looking like the robot who accompanied Michael Rennie in the brilliant black and white sci-fi movie, *The Day The Earth Stood Still*. If you get a chance to see a rerun on TV, don't miss it. Failing that, you can get some idea of a robotic alien from C3PO in *Star Wars*.

Fleshy Robot

This thing looks and acts like a robot, except that it doesn't have a metallic body or skin. How do you act like a robot? Watch any 1950s B movie and you'll get the idea: you move clumsily and stiffly and ... talk ... like ... this ... all ... the ... time. (Fleshy robots aren't the only aspect of the flying-saucer phenomenon that seem a lot like a 1950s B movie.) It's as if somebody created a biological machine in the (very rough) shape of a human and programmed it extremely badly.

Giant

This can look like a cross between a Grey and a Human, but there are, in fact, several types of giant aliens, some of which look more like the Animalian type than anything else. The important characteristic isn't looks at all, but, as you might imagine, size. Giant aliens are BIG.

Avian

This is another category that includes a lot of different-looking creatures. Some are bat-like humanoids. Some are vaguely reptilian. Some have wings and are capable of flight, like the near demonic 'Mothman' that formed the factual basis of the movie *The Mothman Prophecies*, starring Richard Gere.

Short Non-Grey

You can see from the spindly body and small stature where the 'Grey' bit of the classification comes from. But this alien is a far cry from the Classic Grey. In point of fact, these small aliens seem to have more in common with folklore reports of fairies or 'Little People' than they do with space people. Some researchers think we might be dealing with a Grey/Human hybrid here – something that ties in both with the old idea of changelings (fairy children) and the modern abductee reports of breeding experiments involving humans and aliens.

Non-Classics

This is a catch-all category for aliens that don't fit conveniently into any of the more general categories. The illustrations are all artist impressions of various reported alien sightings. I know you'll be curious, so they appeared, in order, in:

Nebraska,
U.S.A., 1967

Essex,
England, 1974

New York State,
U.S.A., 1985

Victoria,
Australia, 1993.

Washington State,
U.S.A., 1995

Physical and Apparitional

Physical and Apparitional are categories that could strictly speaking apply, one way or another, to any of the aliens we've been examining so far – and any you're ever likely to meet in your UFO-hunting career. Most witnesses claim the aliens they've seen were really, truly physically present, as solid as you or I and twice as ugly. But even these physical-seeming aliens are sometimes able to pass through closed doors and thick walls – a talent that would make you suspect they might be illusions, hallucinations or possibly holograms. A few other aliens have presented themselves in a much less physical form, appearing rather like ghosts or phantoms and hence would be categorised as apparitional.

NINETEEN

INTERVIEWING
WITNESSES

This may come as a huge shock to you, but even as a UFO hunter, your chances of meeting an alien are fairly slim. (But not entirely zero: people who take an active interest in the saucers seem to attract more encounters than the population average.) On the other hand, your chances of meeting somebody who claims to have seen an alien are quite high. In these circumstances, you need to know how to interview UFO witnesses, contact witness or abduction victims in a way that will extract enough information for you to decide whether the experience was genuine. Here's how you should go about it:

> First, investigate the witnesses. Try to find out as much as you can about their backgrounds, character and past history. Use the following checklist:
>
> ➤ **Is your witness of good character?** Sounds pompous, I know, but decent, honest, upright citizens are more likely to tell you the truth than the guy who tries to flog you 'fallen off

the back of a lorry' goods. Try to find out your witness's reputation. If the word on the street is that they need to be watched, you may have problems.

➤ **Does your witness have a history of mental illness?** You really do need to be careful about this one. Many investigators have a hideously bad habit of lumping mental illnesses together as if they were all the same thing. They aren't; and there are several forms of mental illness that will make not one whit of difference to the reliability of a witness report. A nervous breakdown, for example, doesn't make you see either aliens or flying saucers. Neither does a psychotic personality (although it might make you strangle a nosy investigator.) What you're looking for here is a history of hallucinations, which can take the form of things seen in the sky or alien beings, or a lying pathology that makes you pretend you did.

➤ **Does your witness have a history of substance abuse?** That's a polite way of asking if he's into drink or drugs. Here again you have to be careful. Although many people will meet a claim of, "I've seen a flying saucer" with the question, "Were you drunk at the time?" The plain fact is that drink does not cause you to see things until you reach the last stages of alcoholism. What it often does is cause you to exaggerate. Some drugs, by contrast do cause you to hallucinate. Both these factors need to be taken into account when evaluating a witness statement.

➤ **Does your witness have any motive for lying about a saucer or alien sighting?** Is she going to make money by selling her story to the newspapers or writing a sensational book? Is she desperate for publicity? Does she like attention? Does she believe an alien contact will give her a romantic aura? You're going to have to make some judgements here. There are people who crave publicity and attention and there are people who would prefer to die rather than step into the limelight. Which category does your witness fall into?

➤ **Is your witness a habitual liar?** This one is a lot more tricky than it sounds. Habitual liars, who lie about anything or everything without motive, are fortunately rare. So rare, in fact, that most of us forget they exist at all. They are often very charming, so you will have a tendency to like (and hence believe) them. The lack of any motive for lying lends a high degree of credibility to their stories. Most of the time you only realise you're dealing with a habitual liar through experience. As an investigator, your best bet is to ask their friends what sort of person they are.

➤ **Is your witness a practical joker?** It's a sad comment on the state of the world, but there really are people out there who think it's absolutely hilarious to fool an up-and-coming UFO hunter like yourself. A witness with a history of practical joking is suspect in anybody's book.

It has to be said that a mad, drunk, villainous, lying joker with a three-book publishing contract could *still* see a genuine UFO, but get real, you have to examine his report a lot more carefully than you might otherwise have done. What lawyers call the burden of proof varies with the circumstances. But once you're reasonably sure your witness is reliable, you can turn your attention to the story.

The first thing to do is get it down properly. This isn't somebody telling you the plot of their favourite movie – it's the raw material for your investigation of a very serious phenomenon. You might even want to pass on the information to an official body or your local UFO organisation. So you need to be sure you don't miss anything important and it's always useful to keep your records in a logical and standardised format. To help you with this, I've created two special report forms, which you're welcome to copy and use.

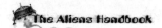
UFO Report Form

Date: ....

Time: ....

Location: ....

UFO type:

Please tick one:

Small disc ☐	Large disc ☐	Cigar-shaped ☐
Globe ☐	Bell-shaped ☐	Triangular ☐
Flying Cross ☐	Other ☐	

Appearance

Shape ....

Size ....

Colour ....

Brightness ....

Transparency ....

Ease of visibility ....

How long in
sight ....

Sighting conditions

Visibility ....

Lighting ....

Weather ....

 19

Behaviour

Movement ....

Sound ....

Other ....

Description

Please write a detailed description of the UFO. Use a
separate sheet of paper if necessary.

....

....

....

....

....

....

....

Sketch UFO here:

19

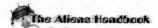

General

Prior reports in this area?	Yes/No
Were you actively UFO spotting?	Yes/No
Did sighting lead to alien contact?	Yes/No

Any Other Associated Phenomena

....

....

....

....

....

Additional Comments

....

....

....

....

Witnessed by:

Name ....

Address ....

....

....

Name ....

Address ....

....

....

Name ....

Address ....

....

....

Alien Contact Report Form

Date: ....

Time: ....

Location: ....

Alien type:

Please tick one:

Human	☐	Grey	☐	Reptilian	☐
Amphibian	☐	Insectoid	☐	Avian	☐
Humanoid	☐	Giant	☐	Other	☐
Fleshy Robot	☐	Metallic Robot	☐		

Contact conditions

Visibility ....

Lighting ....

Weather ....

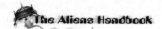

Description

Please write a detailed description of the alien, including colour, size and skin type. Use a separate sheet of paper if necessary.

....

....

....

....

....

....

....

Sketch Alien here:

19

General

Prior reports in this area?	Yes/No
Were you UFO spotting?	Yes/No
Did the aliens communicate with you?	Yes/No

If so...

Was communication verbal or telepathic?

....

....

....

Please write down what was said. (Use separate sheet if necessary.)

....

....

....

....

....

....

....

Did the alien(s) abduct you?	Yes/No

If so...

Please describe the vessel into which you were taken. (Use separate sheet if necessary.)

....

....

....

....

....

....

Please describe in detail what happened to you. (Use separate sheet if necessary.)

....

....

....

....

....

....

Did you lose memory of these
events afterwards?   Yes/No

Did you require hypnotic regression
to prompt your recall?   Yes/No

Prior to this experience did you
believe in alien visitors?   Yes/No

Additional Comments

....

....

....
....
....
....
....

Witnessed by:

Name   ....

Address   ....

        ....

        ....

        ....

Name   ....

Address   ....

        ....

        ....

        ....

Name   ....

Address   ....

        ....

        ....

        ....

19

Use one or both those forms to guide you on the sort of information you need. To get the information, you'll have to seek out and interview witnesses who claim to have seen a flying saucer or met up with an alien. To find them, keep your ears open and watch the newspapers – particularly local newspapers, which often carry reports that never get into the nationals. Subscribe to any UFO news periodical in your district.

Once you have located your witnesses, approach them politely for an interview. Write or phone, introduce yourself and ask if you might call to talk to them about their experience. Don't be shy about what you're up to, but don't try to inflate your importance either. Simply say you're investigating UFOs and/or alien contacts and, if necessary, guarantee their name will not be used in any report you may make public.

If you're granted an interview, turn up on time and do, for heaven's sake, try to look neat. I know it's a bore, but it reassures people and puts them at their ease which means they'll talk to you more freely.

The secret of a successful interview is quiet sympathy. Alien contactees have been through disturbing, sometimes very frightening, experiences and even those who have done no more than spot a flying saucer are usually worried about ridicule. Let them know you have an open mind (if you *don't* have an open mind you shouldn't be a UFO hunter) and they will talk to you more freely.

Ask your questions, keep your mouth shut and *listen*. Don't argue with their opinions, however mad or stupid they may appear to you. Make notes or use a tape recorder (with the witness's permission) since you can never rely entirely on memory if you want an accurate interview. If you're not clear about something, ask questions until you are.

Only after you've collected the story, should you evaluate it. It's important to remember that your witness can honestly believe what he's saying without its being true. For example, the 'flying saucer' he saw could actually have been a shooting star, or the 'alien' he met might just be somebody on the way to a *Star Trek* convention. So while you might accept the story, you must never automatically accept your witness's *interpretation*. In our next chapter you'll find some useful tips on how to go about analysing reports so you can draw your own conclusions.

TWENTY

THE 'RAEL' McCOY?

On the morning of December 13, 1973, a French magazine journalist named Claude Vorilhon was driving to his office in Clermont-Ferrand when an impulse seized him to skip work for a while in order to visit the extinct Puy-de-Lassolas volcano in the Auvergne. It was a cool, misty morning. Vorilhon parked his car and walked to the top of the volcano which gave him a spectacular view of Clermont-Ferrand. He stood for a moment contemplating the ancient history of the district and then he walked back down to his car.

Before climbing into the vehicle, Vorilhon took a last look back at the volcano and saw, at that moment, a flashing red light moving in the sky towards him. It looked a lot like the sort of light you get on a helicopter, but there was no sound of any aircraft and as the light got closer, he could see it was on the underside of a disc-shaped craft about 7 metres in diameter and 2.5 metres in height. There was an

extremely bright white light on the top.

The saucer dropped to a height of about 2 metres, then hovered as a hatch opened in the underside and a staircase slid out to reach the ground. A small, white-robed humanoid emerged. The creature stood about over a metre tall with long, dark hair, almond-shaped eyes and a pale green skin. It spoke smoothly to Vorilhon in French and later claimed to speak every other Earth language just as fluently.

On the visitor's invitation, Vorilhon followed it into the saucer where the creature told him it was a member of an extra-terrestrial race known as the Elohim. Vorilhon had been chosen to receive a special message from the Elohim because he came from France, the 'country where democracy was born'. To this end, he was asked to return for further briefing sessions. Vorilhon agreed to do so and did indeed return to the volcano for the next five days, meeting with the strange visitor for about an hour each morning. Over the period, he learned something quite remarkable.

According to the alien, humanity was not the product of evolution. At a time in the distant past, Earth was visited by an intelligent species from another planet who literally created the first humans using genetic engineering techniques. These extra-terrestrials were the Elohim, the same race of creatures as Vorilhon's messenger.

This scientific creation was actually recorded in the Bible (and in other religious traditions) but mistranslated and misunderstood. The Elohim were thought of as God and the creation as a supernatural event. But the word translated as 'God' in modern versions of the

20

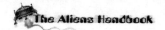

Book of Genesis was 'Elohim,' an ancient Hebrew term which means 'those who came from the sky.'

On their home planet, the Elohim developed an advanced biological technology which enabled them to create life using basic DNA coding. As a spacefaring race they combed the universe looking for a suitably isolated planet to continue their biological experiments in an uncontaminated environment. Eventually they found Earth and established laboratories in what is now known as the Middle East. In these labs they created plants, animals and finally humans – the humans were based on the DNA patterns of the Elohim themselves.

The early humans were housed in the laboratories, comfortably sheltered, fed and looked after by their alien creators. But it was quickly discovered that the new race possessed a remarkably aggressive streak and soon became more trouble than it was worth. The humans were finally thrown out of the laboratories to make their own way in the world as best they could. A distorted memory of all this – creation in the creator's image, loss of a comfortable paradise – forms the basis of the Biblical story of the Garden of Eden.

Some male Elohim were attracted to human women and interbreeding occurred, another event Vorilhon's alien insisted was recorded in the Bible. The result was a number of alien-humans who became heroes and individuals of huge importance in the early history of humanity. All major prophets, including Moses, Buddha, Jesus and Mohammed were of this alien-human stock … as was Vorilhon himself, the Elohim visitor revealed.

Vorilhon was then given a new name – Rael – and told to spread the message of humanity's origins throughout the world. To do so, he was to publish the alien's words in a book and also to form an international movement. The Elohim promised that members of his race would come to Earth again to meet with world leaders and make gifts of beneficial technology – but not until there was world peace and an Elohim Embassy was built for them in Jerusalem.

Rael did as he was told, published several books about his encounter and established the International Raelian Movement, which today claims some 40,000 members. The movement has raised substantial sums of money to build the Elohim Embassy in Jerusalem, but at time of writing (2005) has so far failed to obtain permission from the Israeli authorities to do so. In a controversial and highly publicised venture, the Raelian Movement has since 1997 taken an active interest in cloning (duplicating life through genetic engineering) – which Rael believes holds out the hope of personal immortality. The movement even claims to have achieved the world's first human clone. This case study is quite genuine. You can find out more about the Raelians by logging on to **http://www.rael.org**. But how would you go about analysing it as a UFO hunter?

The story as told sounds pretty fantastic, but you need to keep an open mind – *all* UFO contact reports sound pretty fantastic. Before we go on to the alien's message, it's useful to examine the details of the original encounter. Vorilhon himself was no down-and-out desperately seeking publicity to make himself feel important. He was a professional man with a good job as a journalist in a racing car magazine. His decision to miss work that morning was spontaneous: he had no thought of flying saucers or alien contact in his mind.

He was still not thinking about flying saucers while standing on the volcano. If his account is to be believed – and there seems little reason why it should not be – he was musing on the ancient geological history of the district. Even when he saw the flashing light, he had no thought of UFOs. It was only when it approached him closely that he realised he was looking at something very odd. So far Vorilhon's experience is typical of many flying-saucer sightings. This does not necessarily mean he was telling the truth about it, but it does at least form a consistent part of the overall UFO phenomenon. Even the extended stairway and the small, almond-eyed alien is

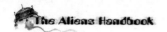

consistent – you can read very similar reports in dozens of other contact cases.

Where Vorilhon parts company with many other contact reports is in the nature of his message. While many early contactees reported that their alien visitors were concerned with the welfare of humanity, none that I'm aware of claimed to be the creators of the human race. If you are a firm believer in mainstream religion, chances are you accept that the creator of the human race (and everything else for that matter) was God. If you have a scientific bent, you probably believe humanity arrived on the planet as the result of several million years of evolution (long process of development). Neither picture leaves much room for the prehistoric appearance of Little Green Men.

All the same, while Charles Darwin's Theory of Evolution is accepted by a majority of scientists today, many have pointed out that there are problems with it; and one or two even believe these problems are so severe that they cast doubt on the theory as a whole.

Curiously enough, one of the problems is the size of your brain. Human brain size made an enormous leap at some point in our evolutionary history and nobody is at all sure why. In Darwin's theory, a sudden change (mutation) will spread through the species only if it proves useful for survival. Suppose you were a tiger who happened to be born with longer claws. Your long claws help you kill more game and survive while less fortunate tigers died off. Consequently, you live long enough to breed. Your offspring will inherit your longer claws and pass the useful mutation on to their offspring in turn, until long claws spreads throughout the whole tiger community. However, if you happened to be born with no legs, the chances of your surviving beyond a cub would be very limited. You would not pass the mutation to your offspring and so legless tigers would never become the norm.

All this is clear enough, but when you think about the big brain mutation, confusion creeps in. We think of the big brain as associated with intelligence, which is certainly a favourable mutation, but the fact remains that there are creatures on this planet with brains many times the size of yours – the blue whale, for example – who still haven't figured out the two-times table. Worse still, as we are continually told, humans make use of only about 10% of their overall brain. The remaining 90% just sits there podging.

But if 90% of your big brain serves no useful evolutionary function, why did it survive to spread throughout the species? The human brain, which allowed Darwin to figure out his Theory of Evolution, does not fit easily into the evolutionary picture. It should not have appeared in our species at all. You'd almost be tempted to think that something *interfered* with the process of human evolution, perhaps using genetic engineering techniques to change the DNA so that a whole new species was produced…

If you hold to the religious viewpoint, problems emerge as well – especially if your belief system is based on the Bible tradition. The Book of Genesis describes how God created the heavens and the Earth along with all its flora and fauna, including humanity. But that's a description in translation. In the original Hebrew of the Genesis story, the word translated as 'God' is actually *Elohim*, just as Vorilhon claimed.

Furthermore, *Elohim* is a very curious word in that it combines a masculine root, *El* (which means 'God') with a feminine plural. So despite what you read in your Bible, *Elohim* should never have been translated as 'God' at all. A more accurate translation would be 'gods and goddesses.' In the religious mythology of virtually every culture on the planet, gods, goddesses, angels etc., are all associated with the sky. (You always go *up* to heaven.) So the Bible actually does support Vorilhon's statement that advanced (godlike) male and female creatures from the sky were involved in the Creation.

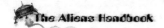

Does this mean Vorilhon really does have inside information direct from the creators of humanity? Not quite. First of all, an alien contact isn't the only place he could have obtained all this. Biblical scholars have long known of the inconsistencies in the Creation story and many scientists realise there are holes in the Theory of Evolution. Also the idea of the Elohim as extra-terrestrials has been put forward by several best-selling authors like Erich Von Daniken and Zacharia Sitchen.

So, like so many analyses of flying-saucer contacts, this one, for all its intriguing aspects, must remain in doubt. Unless, of course, the Elohim make good on their offer to talk to international leaders. But if they continue to insist on world peace before that happens, we may have a long time to wait.

TWENTY ONE

RECOVERING
MEMORIES

One of the most sinister aspects of many – in fact most – alien abduction reports is the claim that the aliens can and do interfere with the memories of their abductees. But the interference is far from perfect. Some victims are left with an uneasy suspicion that something weird happened to them. Others even start to recall certain things. But for most, the only way to get a clear detailed picture of their experience is through hypnosis.

As a UFO hunter, there is a strong likelihood that you'll be involved with hypnosis at some stage. What happens to you during hypnosis is that your awareness changes. As the process gets underway, you find yourself becoming comfortably relaxed; and soon so comfortably relaxed that your whole body begins to feel extremely heavy. This heaviness increases until you feel you can hardly move or that moving just isn't worth the effort. You may find your mind drifting in an easy, dreamy way. If you're like most subjects, you'll find the whole experience very, very pleasant.

While all this is going on, an odd thing happens. The voice of the hypnotist starts to become important to you, until, after a while, it seems to be just about the most important thing in the whole wide world. At this point, your eyes are probably closed, not because you're asleep, but because your eyelids are so heavy you just can't keep them open. The voice of the hypnotist is now your only contact with the outside world.

Contrary to what a great many people believe, you do not lose consciousness. You are aware, more or less, what is going on at all times. It's just that you don't really care very much about it. You are in the process of handing over all responsibility to the hypnotist. He or she will take care of you. He or she will deal with anything that arises.

(Since there are hypnotic subjects who will swear to you that they *did* lose consciousness, I'd better take a moment at this point to mention something called *post-hypnotic amnesia*. This is an impressive term that simply means people who are hypnotised almost always forget what happened during the trance once they come out of it. This leaves them with the impression that they must have been unconscious during the session. But if steps are taken to prevent post-hypnotic amnesia, the subject will remember being awake throughout.)

You may not realise it, but by this stage you are functioning at a different level of awareness to your normal conscious state. One of the biggest differences is that you are far more open to suggestion, provided it comes from the hypnotist. If, for example, the hypnotist told you in your normal waking state that the blue shirt you were wearing was actually pink, you'd shrug it off, possibly decide he was joking, stupid or colour blind. If he made the same suggestion while you were in trance, you'd believe him. If you were in deep trance, you'd actually see the blue shirt as pink.

For deep trance subjects, there is virtually no limit to the persuasive power of the hypnotist. He can make you feel, taste, smell, hear or see things that just aren't there. He can make you believe you are in another country, perhaps busily engaged in an unlikely occupation like pop singing or skiing down Everest. He can convince you that you have become your own mother – a scary thought – or the King

21

of Spain. All of this you will experience as if it were *literally* true and act accordingly.

You can see at once that hypnosis could do a lot of good. If, for example, you were in a lot of pain from a broken toe, the hypnotist could tell you the pain was draining away … which, of course, it would. In fact, since the hypnotist seems to speak directly to your unconscious mind, hypnosis can be used to tackle conditions like allergies, muscle cramps, stress, asthma, warts and so on. No wonder so many doctors took an interest.

One of them, during the 1880s, was an Austrian physician named Sigmund Freud. He saw a demonstration of hypnosis while on a visit to France and was impressed by the hope it held out for treating mental disorders. When he returned home to Vienna he began to use it himself and discovered something very important to every UFO hunter – hypnosis helped people recall disturbing events they had until then completely forgotten.

If you find a UFO witness who believes he may have been abducted (but can remember nothing at all of the event) it may be worthwhile, if your witness agrees, to seek the help of a good hypnotist.[1] You'll have to find one the subject will trust if you want to be sure of results. Typically what will happen is something like this: the subject will be invited to relax in comfort and to fix his gaze on some object, usually held above eye level. The hypnotist will begin to talk to him in a calm, quiet voice, suggesting that his relaxation is increasing and his eyes are growing tired. Once the subject's eyes really do show signs of tiring, the hypnotist will suggest they close. By this point, the subject's body will probably have grown quite limp and his breathing deepened. He has passed into a trance state.

Once this happens, the hypnotist can start on a process of regression, which involves suggesting that the subject goes back in time remembering clearly various events that occurred along the

---

1 Or do the job yourself. Hypnosis isn't that difficult to learn – I managed it at the age of nine.

135

way. It's relatively easy to pick out events like birthdays, Christmas, Easter or whatever, that will give the subject useful signposts in this process. Once regression is firmly established, the subject can be gently led towards the time and place of the suspected abduction. Skilfully done, regression can lead to the revealing of the entire forgotten incident.

This all seems straightforward enough, but there are problems. First of all, the hypnotist has to be extremely careful not to *suggest* any of the evidence he is trying to uncover. This is something you need to watch for very closely, since it can be done so subtly that not even the hypnotist realises it is happening. Take a look at the following fragment of dialogue:

Hypnotist: I want you to go back to the day you saw the flying saucer land.

Subject: Yes.

Hypnotist: I'd like you to describe the craft.

Subject: It was about 7 metres in diameter, made from some sort of silver-coloured metal.

Hypnotist: With windows?

Subject: Yes.

Hypnotist: Did any creature come out of the saucer?

Subject: Yes. A ramp came down and a small being in a silver suit came out. It had a large head, large dark eyes and almost no nose or mouth.

Hypnotist: You thought this was an alien being from another planet?

Subject: Yes.

On the face of it, that seems like an innocent enough exchange, but in fact every major element of the story was unconsciously suggested by the hypnotist. He began by taking the subject back to 'the day he saw the flying saucer land.' But the subject didn't remember seeing a flying saucer land – he simply suspected he might have been abducted because there was a blank period in his recollection of a particular day.

Once the saucer had been suggested, the subject filled in a classical, but entirely fictitious, description of what he saw, aided by the hypnotist who unwittingly suggested the windows, the presence of a 'creature' and the possibility that the creature was an alien from another planet. Remember that while in trance the subject is unable to reject the hypnotist's suggestions and will always build a supporting fantasy around them if required – which is exactly what is happening in this case.

Closely associated with the problem of suggestibility is the fact that a trance subject is driven to please the hypnotist. This means that if the subject believes the hypnotist wants to hear a story about flying saucers, that's the story he'll get, whether it's true or not. That holds good however careful the actual questioning may be. Subjects aren't (usually) stupid and will easily detect whether the hypnotist is a UFO enthusiast. If he is, the chances of the subject producing a UFO story increase alarmingly.

To make matters worse, the subject will believe his own fiction! The whole process of pleasing the hypnotist and/or reacting to suggestion is all completely unconscious. After only a very few sessions, you'll have a full-blown case of false memory syndrome on your hands. Your subject can have a clear, detailed and permanent recollection of a whole series of events, conversations and experiences that never happened at all.

The only way to guard against this is to approach the investigation from a position of absolute neutrality. You are simply investigating what happened to your subject on a particular date with no expectations whatsoever. Once that is clear to both of you, you'll find out the truth of his experience … whether or not it involves Little Green Men in their flying saucers.

TWENTY TWO

WHAT TO DO IF
YOU'RE ABDUCTED

If you go looking for a tiger, you need to know what to do if you find one. From most accounts, UFO aliens aren't as dangerous as tigers, but there have been pilots killed by flying saucers and some alien abductions have a nightmare quality you would definitely want to avoid. So now you've decided to become a UFO hunter, is there anything you can do to help keep yourself out of trouble?

Let's start with the saucers themselves. Since the first modern sightings in the 1940s, there's been little evidence of hostile intent. Saucers don't generally shoot at you or drop bombs on your home. But that's not to say they can't be dangerous. Several pilots have died while chasing UFOs. Most have crashed. A few have simply disappeared, which may just mean the wreckage of their planes was never found, or may point to something just as sinister and a lot more weird. Either way, the lesson is simple: if you're up in a plane, it's fine to watch a UFO, it's even fine to photograph a UFO, but it's dumb to get too close to a UFO. Keeping your distance could save your life.

You should also keep your distance from any UFO you may discover on the ground, although that's such an exciting prospect you could find the rule hard to follow. The good news is that if you don't follow it, you're less likely to be killed than you would be if you approached a UFO in flight.

There is, unfortunately, the possibility you will be injured. Various reports associate saucers (and saucer landings in particular) with radiation. Witnesses have suffered burns – sometimes severe burns – or mysterious skin rashes. There have also been reports of dizziness, disorientation and black-outs, all fortunately temporary, but no less unpleasant for that. The official 'flying-saucers-are-figments' policy has meant there are no long-term studies of UFO radiation effects, so exposure may only be a passing inconvenience. But you can't be sure of this and until you are, the only real safeguard is to keep your distance.

UFO aliens are a different matter. However seriously you're minding your own business, they have a nasty habit of coming to you. They can even turn up in your bedroom, for heaven's sake – and pass through solid walls! Is there anything you can do to protect yourself?

There is ... but this is where things are going to get a little complicated. All the evidence suggests that UFO abductions are not *exactly* what they appear to be. Some abductions have been witnessed by people not directly involved. Others affect a single person, with his or her companions reporting that nothing at all happened. Huge UFOs can land without crushing so much as a blade of grass. Others leave visible signs – including scorch marks and changes in ground chemistry – of their presence.

Many Ufologists accept part of this evidence to 'prove' that flying-saucer aliens have a real, physical presence. Others accept a different part to 'prove' the creatures are all in the witnesses'

imagination. But if you consider *all* the evidence, the only possible conclusion is that the abduction phenomenon is partly physical and partly imaginary ... and that the imaginary part has some very different characteristics to what we normally think of as imagination.

You know what imagination is, of course – it's that pleasant inner world you enter when you daydream. You probably think of it as something you create. Now, let's look at UFOs. They're physically real, because they show up on radar, a detection system that works by bouncing waves off physical objects. But they manoeuvre, appear and disappear in ways that are quite impossible for physical craft, which means they *can't* be physical.

In abductions, the contradiction is even more obvious. The experience *feels* as if it's happening in the ordinary world and sometimes it really is. But at other times it clearly isn't. Yet even when it seems to have been a vivid hallucination, those involved can sometimes 'bring back' physical evidence in the form of implants.

It's as if human imagination isn't just pictures you make up inside your head, but some sort of gateway into another reality. And there are creatures that seem to be able to walk through it. These creatures are shaped by popular imagination so that today they're most likely to appear with small, spindly bodies, large heads and huge black eyes, but they've probably taken on other forms in the past… and been given names we now associate with creatures from myths.

This is just a theory, of course, but it's a theory that allows you to do something to defend yourself against abduction. First, tackle the physical side. A common characteristic of almost every close encounter is an interruption of the local electricity supply. Any device that gives you audible warning of a power cut (like Desmond Leslie's UFO detector) will also warn you of an impending abduction.

Next, remember that if the phenomenon really has been with us over many centuries, as seen in the folklore of various cultures, then our ancestors are reported to have found ways of dealing with unwanted visitors that were generally considered extremely reliable. Several of them remain well worth using today, including:

> **A ring of salt around yourself or your bed.**

Salt was believed to have such purifying power that demons and other supernatural creatures could not bear to cross over it. This belief may well have arisen from the ancient use of this substance to deter aliens.

> **A liberal sprinkling of herbs traditionally used to repel unwanted visitors.**

These include garlic, yarrow and pennyroyal; but avoid pennyroyal if anyone in the house happens to be pregnant as it can cause the loss of the unborn baby.

> **Light has long been believed to be troublesome to supernatural creatures and, indeed, most abductions are reported as occurring during the hours of darkness.**

Turning on a bright light may repel an alien and a well-lighted space could deter any visitation in the first place. But remember electrical power may go down, so use light that doesn't need it. (Batteries will sometimes work when mains power fails, but not always.)

> **The single substance most disliked by the 'faerie folk' is traditionally recorded to be iron.**

Use iron nails and iron filings. Some authorities suggest you carry an iron cross or crucifix, if you are Christian; or the equivalent symbol of your own religion if not.

22

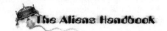

The mention of religious symbols brings in a difficult aspect of abduction protection. It may be that the *frame of mind* of the victim has an influence on what can happen. Consequently prayer (assuming you're a believer) can be a protective influence, as can visualising yourself surrounded by a circle of white light.

Associated with all this is the strong suspicion that certain abductions – notably those which carry their victims through solid walls – have something in common with out-of-body experience. This is a phenomenon, experienced by about one in four people at some time during their lives, in which consciousness seems to move out of the physical body and move around the world like a ghost. The experience of an OOBE is not at all ghostly, however, and can easily be confused with physical reality.

If the suspicion is correct and there really is a connection between OOBEs and some abductions, then the process can be cut short by returning consciousness to the physical body. Usually this requires no more than a total refusal to cooperate with the abductors and a determination to return to the body.

AFTERWORD

Of course, you might actually *enjoy* being abducted. If so, an American company – Alien Abductions Incorporated – can arrange it for you. According to their promotional material…

When you choose an AAI Abduction Experience our doctors, hypnotists, and memory implant technicians work with you in pre-abduction orientation sessions to customize one of our hundreds of stock abductions to suit your personal taste.

Good luck … and good hunting!

INDEX